OXFORD
UNIVERSITY PRESS

ASPIRE
SUCCEED
PROGRESS

Complete
Computer Science
for Cambridge IGCSE® & O Level

Revision Guide

Alison Page
David Waters

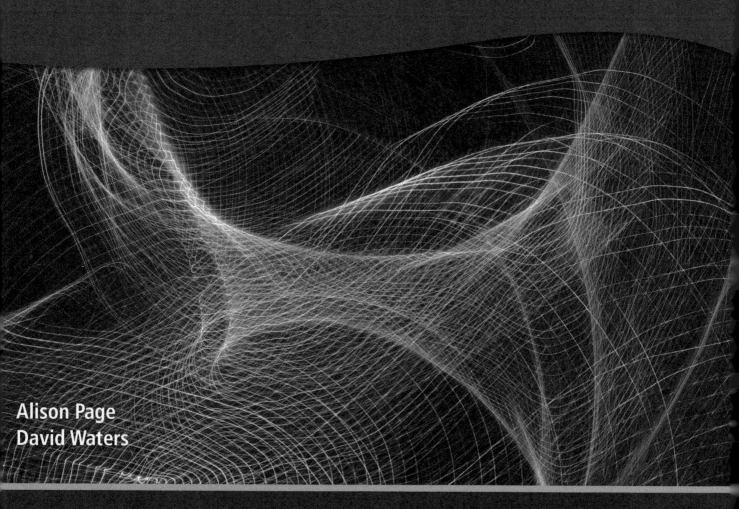

Oxford excellence for Cambridge IGCSE® & O Level

OXFORD

OXFORD
UNIVERSITY PRESS

Great Clarendon Street, Oxford, OX2 6DP, United Kingdom

Oxford University Press is a department of the University of
Oxford. It furthers the University's objective of excellence in
research, scholarship, and education by publishing worldwide.
Oxford is a registered trade mark of Oxford University Press in
the UK and in certain other countries

British Library Cataloguing in Publication Data
Data available

978-0-19-836725-3

7 9 10 8

Paper used in the production of this book is a natural,
recyclable product made from wood grown in sustainable
forests. The manufacturing process conforms to the
environmental regulations of the country of origin.

Printed and bound by CPI Group (UK) Ltd, Croydon, CR0 4YY

Acknowledgements
The publishers would like to thank the following for
permissions to use their photographs:

Cover: John Lund / Getty Images

p53: Aleph Studio / Shutterstock; Anatoly Vartanov /
Shutterstock; Bloomua / Shutterstock; p96: Alison Page

Artwork by Q2A Media Services Pvt. Ltd., MPS and OUP

Although we have made every effort to trace and contact all
copyright holders before publication this has not been possible
in all cases. If notified, the publisher will rectify any errors or
omissions at the earliest opportunity.

Contents

1 Data representation

This page summarises what you will learn about data representation. Tick the boxes on this page when you are confident you have learned each item.

1.1 Binary systems

TICK THE BOX WHEN YOU HAVE LEARNED:

- [ ] what binary data and binary numbers are
- [ ] what "bits" and "bytes" are
- [ ] what denary numbers are
- [ ] how position changes the value of a digit in a number
- [ ] how to count upwards in binary
- [ ] how to convert binary numbers into denary numbers
- [ ] how to convert denary numbers into binary numbers.

1.2 Hexadecimal

TICK THE BOX WHEN YOU HAVE LEARNED:

- [ ] what hexadecimal numbers are
- [ ] the 16 hexadecimal digits
- [ ] how to convert hexadecimal to denary
- [ ] how to convert denary to hexadecimal
- [ ] how to convert binary to hexadecimal
- [ ] how to convert hexadecimal to binary
- [ ] the advantages of hexadecimal
- [ ] the main uses of hexadecimal in computer science.

1.3 Data storage

TICK THE BOX WHEN YOU HAVE LEARNED:

- [ ] how text and numbers are stored on the computer
- [ ] the different ways to store image files
- [ ] the relationship between image quality and file size
- [ ] how sounds and video are stored on the computer
- [ ] file formats used for images, sounds and video
- [ ] the factors that improve the quality of audio and video
- [ ] the difference between lossless and lossy compression
- [ ] ways of compressing files and the effect on quality.

1.1 Binary systems

Binary data

A computer is an electronic machine. The data inside the computer is stored as electronic on/off signals. These binary signals can be used to represent many different forms of data. These signals are dynamic – they are always changing. By changing the electronic signals the computer transforms the data. This transformation is called processing. Everything that you will learn on a computer science course arises from these key facts.

Fact check

What is a computer? A computer is a machine for data processing. The computer processes data electronically. A computer stores and processes data using electrical switches. The switches can be on (conduct electricity) or off (no electricity).

Binary data: "Binary" means anything that can be in exactly two states, for example electrical switches that can be on or off. All data inside the computer is stored in binary form. We represent this data using 1s and 0s to stand for "on" and "off".

Forms of data: Binary can be used to represent many different forms of data:

- numbers, text
- images
- sound
- video.

> ### Check your readiness
> You should understand why computers are important and useful to us. What does binary mean? Can you explain why computer science students learn about binary numbers?

Bits and bytes

Data is held inside the computer in binary form. We represent the on/off signals using 1s and 0s (bits). Bits are organised into groups of eight called bytes. Computer memory and storage are measured in bytes. Active computer memory is also called RAM. A computer with large RAM can process more data, more quickly than one with less RAM.

Fact check

What are bits and bytes? A 1 or 0 is a "binary digit". This is shortened to "bit". Inside the computer, bits are organised in groups of eight. A group of eight bits is called a byte. When we write a binary number we write it as a complete byte. If there aren't enough bits we add 0s at the start to make a complete byte:

```
0 0 0 1 1 1 0 1
```

You need to know:
- what binary data and binary numbers are
- that computers process data to make information
- that this processing occurs in digital form.

Key terms

Data: "raw" facts and figures

Information: data that has been organised and transformed to make it more useful

Data processing: turning data into information.

You need to know:
- what "bits" and "bytes" are
- how to measure computer memory using bytes.

Main memory: All data is held as electrical signals inside the computer. The main memory that holds data is called random access memory (RAM). We measure the size of RAM in bytes.

RAM and computer power: RAM is the active memory of the computer. Data can be processed quickly if it is held in RAM. In general, more RAM means a faster and more powerful computer.

Units of measurement: RAM and storage are measured in bytes. A kilobyte is 1024 bytes. A megabyte is 1024 kilobytes. A gigabyte is 1024 megabytes.

Registers: Data processing means data is changed and transformed. This is done by changing the electronic signals that make the data. At the time it is processed, this data is stored in a small area of memory called a register. A register holds just a few bits of data (e.g. 8 bit, 32 bit).

Key terms
Bit: A single binary digit – a 1 or 0
Byte: A group of 8 bits.

Check your readiness

Without looking at your notes or this page, answer these questions. How are bits organised inside the computer? How do we measure the capacity of RAM? What computer applications or games need really fast processing speed? Why does bigger RAM mean a faster computer?

Binary and denary

There are many different number systems. The number system we use in everyday life is called denary or base 10. The denary system has ten digits. Computers use the binary system, which has two digits. The value of a digit in either binary or denary depends on its position in the number.

You need to know:
• what binary and denary numbers are
• how positional values change the significance of digits in numbers.

Fact check

Denary numbers: Something that can be in ten different states is known as denary. Our normal number system is denary. We also call our number system "base 10" and "decimal". Denary numbers use ten digits:

0 1 2 3 4 5 6 7 8 9

Place value in denary: The same digit can represent different values in a denary number. The value of a digit depends on its position in the number. The value on the right is units. As you move left, each position is ten times bigger. In the denary number 3086 the 3 stands for three times a thousand.

Key terms
Denary: Base 10; a number system with ten digits
Binary: Base 2; a number system with two digits.

Thousands	Hundreds	Tens	Units
3	0	8	6

Place value in binary: Binary has only two digits (bits). The value of a bit depends on its position in the number. The value on the right is units. As you move left, each position is two times bigger.

In the binary number 1000, the 1 stands for one times eight.

Eights	Fours	Twos	Units
1	0	0	0

Check your readiness

Without looking at your notes or this page, answer these questions. Can you explain the difference between denary and binary? Does your explanation include the number of digits and the place value of digits? Can you identify the value of a binary or denary digit by multiplying the digit by the place value?

Counting in binary

The principles of counting up in denary and binary are the same. You increase the value of the digits in the units column until you have used all the digits. Then you reset the units column to 0 and increase the next largest column by 1. Binary numbers are made of just two digits: 1s and 0s.

You need to know:
- the rules of binary counting
- how to count upwards in binary.

Fact check

Counting in denary: There are ten denary digits (from 0 to 9). When you have counted up to 9 you have run out of digits.

> 9

Reset the units column to 0 and put 1 in the tens column.

> 10

Now continue in this way.

> 99

When you reach 99 you have run out of digits. Reset the tens and digits to 0 and put 1 in the hundreds column.

> 100

The largest number you can make with three digits is 999. What happens next?

Counting in binary: This is just the same as denary, except there are only two digits.

> Count 0
>
> Count 1

Now you have run out of digits. Reset the units column to 0 and put a 1 in the next column (the twos column).

> Count 1 0
>
> Count 1 1

You have run out of digits. Reset the units and twos to zero and put a 1 in the next column (the fours column).

Writing binary number as bytes: Remember that we often add 0s at the left of a binary number to make it up to eight bits (one byte).

Check your readiness

Without looking at your notes or this page, write out the complete series of 8-bit binary numbers starting at 0 0 0 0 0 0 0 0 and ending at 1 1 1 1 1 1 1 1.

Convert binary to denary

Each bit in a byte has a set value depending on its position. The position on the far right is worth 1. Work out the value of each position by multiplying by 2. This creates a table called the binary grid. To work out the value of a binary number put the bits into the binary grid. Add up all values that have a 1 underneath.

You need to know:
- how to convert binary numbers into denary numbers.

Fact check

The binary grid: This shows the position values of each bit in a byte. The bit on the right is worth 1. As you move to the left through the byte, each position is worth double the previous position.

128	64	32	16	8	4	2	1

Convert binary to denary: Put the eight bits of a binary number into the eight columns of the binary grid. Note every value that has a 1 underneath it. Add these values together.

If there are fewer than eight bits in the number: Make sure the number is at the right of the table. Fill up the empty columns on the left with 0s.

16-bit numbers: You can convert a number with more than eight bits. The method is the same. Use this 16-column table.

32 768	16 384	8192	4096	2048	1024	512	256	128	64	32	16	8	4	2	1

You don't have to memorise all the position values in this table. Just start on the right with 1 and multiply each column by 2 as you move to the left.

Check your readiness

Work on your own or with a friend. Write a series of eight bits, mixing 1s and 0s. Use the binary grid to work out the value of the number you have just written. Repeat this as many times as you can until conversion comes easily.

Convert denary to binary

There are several ways to turn denary numbers into binary. The method shown on this page is the reverse of the method you just learned for converting binary to denary. Subtract the values of the binary grid. Put a 1 below each value as you subtract it. All other columns have a 0.

You need to know:
- how to convert denary numbers to binary.

Fact check

The binary grid: To convert a denary number to binary we use the binary grid (position table). This eight-bit grid will convert a denary number from 0 to 255:

128	64	32	16	8	4	2	1

For larger numbers use the 16-bit grid.

Subtraction method: Start at the left of the binary grid (largest values). Find the largest value you can subtract from the number (without going below 0). Put a 1 into the grid below that value and subtract it from the number.

Keep subtracting values and putting 1s into the grid. Stop when you reach 0. Put 0s into any empty columns of the grid. Finally, show the bits without the grid.

Worked example: Convert 40 to binary

$$40 - 32 = 8$$
$$8 - 8 = 0$$

You have subtracted 32 and 8. Put 1 under these values. Fill in the rest of the grid with 0s.

128	64	32	16	8	4	2	1
0	0	1	0	1	0	0	0

Show the bits without the grid. The result is 0 0 1 0 1 0 0 0.

Check your readiness

Work on your own or with a friend. Write any denary number from 0 to 255. Convert it to binary, then back to denary, using the methods you have learned. You should get back to the number you started with. Repeat this until you can do it easily without errors.

1.1 Knowledge test

1. Computers transform data. What do they transform it into and why is this important to us?

2. What does "binary" mean?

3. How do binary numbers differ from denary numbers? Give as many differences as you can.

4. Why do computer science students learn about binary numbers?

5. How is a bit represented inside of RAM?

6. How are bits organised inside the computer?

7. What units do we use to measure the capacity of RAM?

8. Why does more RAM mean a faster computer?

9. Write out the sequence of binary numbers starting at 0 0 0 1 0 0 0 0 and ending at 0 0 0 1 0 1 1 0.

10. Fill in the missing position values in this binary grid.

128						2	1

11. Fill in the missing position values in this binary grid.

32768		8192	4096	2048		512	256	128					2	1

12. Translate these binary numbers into denary. Show your working.
    0 1 1 0 0 0 1 1
    0 0 1 1 1 1 0 0
    1 0 1 1 1 1 0 1
    1 1 0 0 1 1 0 1
    1 0 1 0 1 0 1 0 0 (this is more than one byte).

13. Translate these denary numbers into binary. Show your working.
    81
    106
    217
    290 (this is more than one byte)
    1010 (this is more than one byte).

1.2 Hexadecimal

What is hexadecimal?

Hexadecimal is base 16. Hexadecimal has 16 different digits. Each position value is 16 times bigger than the previous one. Hexadecimal is used in computing because it is easier to convert binary to hexadecimal than to denary. Hexadecimal numbers are easier to read and to write than binary.

Fact check

Hexadecimal digits: Hexadecimal numbers have 16 different digits. The digits 0–9 are the same as denary. There are six more digits:

A = 10

B = 11

C = 12

D = 13

E = 14

F = 15.

Hexadecimal position values: The value of a hexadecimal digit depends on its position value. In this lesson you will study two-digit hexadecimal numbers:

- the right digit = units
- the left digit = 16s.

See the next lesson for longer numbers.

Converting a two-digit hexadecimal number to denary: Convert the digit on the right to denary. Convert the digit on the left to denary and multiply by 16. Add the two values together

Why use hexadecimal? Binary numbers are useful in computer science because computers use binary format. However, binary numbers are hard to read and understand. Hexadecimal numbers are easy to convert into binary. Computer scientists therefore use hexadecimal to represent binary data.

Check your readiness

Work on your own or with a friend. Write any two-digit hexadecimal number. It can include any of the hexadecimal digits 0–9 and A–F. Convert the number to denary. Repeat this practice until you are confident with conversion.

Hexadecimal and denary

By using the values of the 16 hexadecimal digits, and the position values, you can convert between hexadecimal and denary. Multiply hexadecimal digits by position value to convert to denary. Divide a denary number by position value to convert to hexadecimal.

You need to know:
- what hexadecimal numbers are
- how to convert two-digit hexadecimal numbers to denary numbers
- why hexadecimal numbers are used in computer science.

Key term
Hexadecimal: Base 16; a number system with 16 digits.

You need to know:
- how to convert hexadecimal numbers of any length to denary
- how to convert denary numbers to hexadecimal.

Fact check

Converting denary numbers from 0–255 to hexadecimal: Divide the denary number by 16. The result goes in the 16s column. The remainder goes in the units column.

The hexadecimal grid: This grid shows the position values of a four-digit hexadecimal number. You do not need to memorise these position values – simply multiply each number by 16, using a calculator, to get the next number.

4096	256	16	1

Converting hexadecimal to denary (up to four digits): Put the digits of a hexadecimal number into the grid. Multiply the digit value by the position value. Add the values together.

Converting denary numbers above 255 to hexadecimal: Use the hexadecimal grid. Find the biggest value that you can divide by, and put the result of the division under that number. Divide the remainder by the biggest number that you can, and put the result under that number. Continue dividing until you cannot divide any more. Put the final remainder in the units column.

Check your readiness

Work on your own or challenge a friend. Convert denary numbers to hexadecimal and hexadecimal number to denary. Complete as many as you can.

Hexadecimal and binary

There is an exact match between the 16 hexadecimal digits and the first 16 binary numbers. This makes conversion between the two number systems very easy.

You need to know:
- how to convert hexadecimal number to binary
- how to convert binary number to hexadecimal.

Fact check

Exact match: There is an exact match between the 16 hexadecimal digits and the 16 binary numbers from 0 0 0 0 to 1 1 1 1. Every hexadecimal digit matches a group of four bits. There are no remainders or spare bits, which you get with denary conversion.

The conversion table: The conversion table (at the top of page 10) makes it easy to match hexadecimal digits to groups of four bits. If you want to convert numbers and you haven't got a copy of the table, you can easily create it using your skills in binary and hexadecimal counting.

To convert hexadecimal to binary: Write down the digits of the hexadecimal number. Under each digit write the four bits that match that digit. Fit the two groups of four together to make an eight-bit binary number.

```
    5          B
  0 1 0 1    1 0 1 1
  5B = 0 1 0 1 1 0 1 1
```

To convert binary to hexadecimal: Write down the binary number in groups of four bits. If the bits don't split exactly into groups of four then add extra 0s at the start. Under each group of four bits write the matching hexadecimal digit:

```
  1 1 0 0 1 1 1 0
    C       E
  1 1 0 0 1 1 1 0 = CE
```

There is no need to turn the numbers into denary.

Binary	Hexadecimal
0 0 0 0	0
0 0 0 1	1
0 0 1 0	2
0 0 1 1	3
0 1 0 0	4
0 1 0 1	5
0 1 1 0	6
0 1 1 1	7
1 0 0 0	8
1 0 0 1	9
1 0 1 0	A
1 0 1 1	B
1 1 0 0	C
1 1 0 1	D
1 1 1 0	E
1 1 1 1	F

Check your readiness

Work on your own or challenge a friend. Convert binary numbers to hexadecimal and hexadecimal numbers to binary. Complete as many as you can, including large numbers with lots of digits.

How hexadecimal is used

Hexadecimal has many advantages over denary or binary. Hexadecimal gives computer scientists a convenient way to describe the numerical values used in computer science.

You need to know:
- how hexadecimal is used by computer scientists.

Fact check

Why use hexadecimal instead of denary? Hexadecimal matches binary exactly. Conversion is quick and easy.

Why use hexadecimal instead of binary? Hexadecimal is easier to read and understand than binary. It is easier to write a hexadecimal number without making a mistake. It is easier to check your work for errors.

Memory locations: The computer's electronic memory is called RAM. Every location in RAM has its own address. The address is a binary number. We normally use a hexadecimal number to write the memory address.

Machine code: This is a number code system that turns all software instructions into binary numbers. Programmers who write in machine code almost always turn these numbers into hexadecimal. Error messages are also displayed using a hexadecimal code.

24-bit colour: 24 bits means 3 bytes. We use three bytes to represent colours:

• byte 1: the amount of red
• byte 2: the amount of blue
• byte 3: the amount of green.

By mixing red, blue and green in the right proportions we can recreate every colour. Instead of showing the bytes as binary numbers we show them as hexadecimal.

Check your readiness

Without looking at your notes or this page, answer these questions. Can you explain the advantages of hexadecimal over binary? What are the advantages over denary? Can you think of any disadvantages of hexadecimal compared to denary? List two or three uses of hexadecimal in computer science.

1.2 Knowledge test

1. What are the advantages of hexadecimal over binary?
2. What are the advantages of hexadecimal over denary?
3. List two or three uses of hexadecimal in computer science.
4. Convert these two-digit hexadecimal numbers to denary.

   3F

   90

   AD

   D6

5. Convert these denary numbers into two-digit hexadecimal.

   73

   166

   91

   204

6. Convert these longer hexadecimal numbers to denary.

   123

   A1A

7. Convert these longer denary numbers into hexadecimal.

   270

   3072

8. Convert these binary numbers to hexadecimal. The bits are grouped into sets of 4.

   0 0 0 1 0 0 0 1 1 1 1 0

   1 1 1 1 0 0 0 0 1 1 1 1

   1 1 0 1 1 0 1 0 0 1 1 1

9. Convert these hexadecimal numbers to binary.

   BB3

   ABC

   99E

1.3 Data storage

Digital data

All data is held in the computer as on/off signals, which make binary numbers. This electronic system can be used to store whole numbers, fractions and text characters.

Fact check

Whole numbers (integers): Any whole number can be represented in binary. One byte of storage can hold binary numbers equivalent to denary 0–255. For larger numbers the computer uses several bytes linked together.

Fractions (floating point numbers): In the denary system, fractions smaller than 1 can be shown using a decimal point. For example one half is 0.5. In binary, a fraction can be shown in the same way, using a point. In binary one half is 0.1. The computer stores the digits of the number as a whole binary number. The computer uses an extra byte to store the position of the point in the number. This type of number is called a floating point number (or "float" for short).

Text data: Every text character is given a binary code number. The computer stores the code numbers. The most common coding system is ASCII. ASCII has a number code for every keyboard character. Unicode is an extended code system. It has a binary code for all characters, including non-European alphabets and other symbols.

File formats: Different ways of storing data are called formats. Different types of computer file use different formats. A file name usually ends with a three- or four- letter file extension. The file extension tells the computer the format of the data in that file.

Check your readiness

Without looking at your notes or this page, briefly describe how the computer stores whole numbers from 0–255, numbers larger than 255, floating point numbers and text characters.

Digital graphics

Images of all kinds can be stored using binary numbers. There are two methods: bitmap and vector. Each method has advantages and disadvantages.

Fact check

Images and pixels: A computer image is made of pixels ("pixel" is short for "picture element"). A pixel is the smallest part of a picture that can be changed. Computers store images in two completely different ways: bitmap and vector.

Bitmap graphics: In a bitmap file the computer stores the colour of each pixel as a different code number. A large image can have millions of pixels.

The advantages of bitmap graphics are as follows:

- Bitmap graphics are detailed, realistic images.
- Bitmaps files are good for storing photographs and colourful art.

Bitmap graphics also have disadvantages:

- They are large files, because they have millions of numbers, one for each pixel.
- When a bitmap image is expanded, the computer makes all the pixels bigger. The image ends up "pixelated": it looks as if it is made up of large dots.

Vector graphics: A vector image is made up of shapes constructed from lines. The computer uses mathematical formulas to store the size and shape of each element. When you want to see the image, the computer draws all the elements from the stored formulas.

These are the advantages of vector graphics:

- A vector image makes a much smaller file than a bitmap image.
- Vector graphics are sharp, precise and simple.
- When a vector image is expanded, the computer redraws the image to a larger size. The image quality is as good as in the smaller image.

The disadvantage of vector graphics is that they cannot store realistic colour photographs.

Check your readiness

What are the two image formats? Produce a table showing the characteristics, advantages and disadvantages of both formats.

Digital sound and video

Computers can store sounds and moving images. Typically, these are large files. Higher-quality sound and video uses more storage space than lower-quality examples.

You need to know:
- how sounds and moving images are stored in binary form
- the different audio and video formats.

Fact check

Audio files: Audio means "sound". Modern musicians use computers to edit and combine sounds.

Audio formats:

- WAV stores sound accurately and with high quality, but it makes large file sizes.
- MP3 stores sound at lower quality but the file size is smaller.
- MIDI – the computer stores the instructions for making sounds. A MIDI file will be sent to a synthesiser that will make the sounds. MIDI files are quite small. Sound quality depends on the synthesizer.

Uses of the different audio formats:

- WAV is used for high-quality recordings (e.g. CDs and radio broadcasts).
- MP3 is used for lower-quality small recordings (e.g. on MP3 players or for Internet streaming).
- MIDI is used in a recording studio to allow the producer to edit and mix different tracks.

File size and quality: The quality and file size of an audio track depends on:

- sample rate (the number of times the sound changes per second)
- number of channels (mono, stereo, quadraphonic etc.)
- bit depth (the range of sound frequencies used).

It can take 1 megabyte to store only a few seconds of high-quality audio.

Video formats: Video files store sound and moving images. A moving image is made by running still images very fast, giving the appearance of movement. The main video format is MP4. MP4 is like a container that can hold sound, moving images and other content. Video file size depends on the same factors as audio, plus image quality.

Check your readiness

Without looking at your notes or this page, list the main audio and video formats. What are their main features and uses? What factors determine the quality of video and audio files?

Compression

Compression means any method that reduces the size of a file. Most compression is lossy, which means there is some loss of data quality. Lossless compression retains quality while reducing file size.

Fact check

Why compress files? Large files take up a lot of storage space, and they are slower to transmit over the Internet. However, small files tend to be poor quality. This applies to image, audio and video formats. Compression offers a way to keep the high quality, but without the huge file size.

How to compress an image:

- Remove repetition: if there is a big block of the same colour, store one pixel, and the number of repetitions.
- Reduce colour depth: use a smaller selection of colours.
- Reduce image resolution: use fewer larger pixels.

How to compress audio:

- Use fewer channels: (e.g. mono instead of stereo).
- Reduce sample rate: record fewer sound changes per second.
- Reduce bit depth: remove the highest and lowest sounds.

How to compress video:

- Reduce audio quality.
- Reduce image quality.
- Reduce the number of images per second.

You need to know:

- how data can be compressed
- the difference between lossless and lossy compression
- the file types for compressed data.

Key terms

Lossless compression: reduction in the size of a data file with no loss of data quality

Lossy compression: reduction in file size with some loss of quality.

JPG (pronounced "jay-peg"): This is a compressed bitmap format. JPG is a lossy compression method. JPG formats produce fairly good-quality photographs. JPG is a common file format for images on websites.

How to compress a text file:

- Text files can be compressed with no loss of quality (lossless).
- One method is to find repeated words or sections and replace with a code or index.
- Text files may be converted to ZIP or PDF formats.

Check your readiness

Without looking at your notes or this page, describe the two types of file compression. Explain how image and audio files can be compressed. What is the effect on file quality?

1.3 Knowledge test

1. Why does a computer need to use more than one byte to store numbers larger than 255?

2. What are floating point numbers?

3. How does the computer store text characters?

4. How does a bitmap file store an image?

5. What are the advantages and disadvantages of bitmap graphics?

6. How does a vector graphic file store an image?

7. What are the advantages and disadvantages of vector graphics?

8. What type of data is stored in each of the following file formats? Give any other information you know about these formats:
   - WAV
   - MP3
   - MIDI
   - MP4.

9. What factors determine the quality of an audio file?

10. What is the difference between lossless and lossy compression?

11. Explain two ways an image file can be reduced in size.

Exam preparation

1. Use the information contained in topics 1.1 and 1.2 to explain the following:
   a. What binary means
   b. What binary digit means
   c. What hexadecimal means
   d. What hexadecimal digits are.

Exam-style questions

1. a. Convert the following 16 bit binary number to hexadecimal

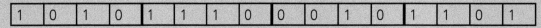

| 1 | 0 | 1 | 0 | 1 | 1 | 1 | 0 | 0 | 0 | 1 | 0 | 1 | 1 | 0 | 1 |

   b. Convert the hexadecimal numbers AB and F7 to binary:

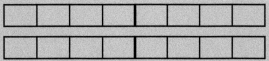

   c. Perform the logical AND function on the two binary numbers from part (b).

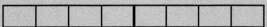

   d. Convert the binary number from part **c** to denary.

2. When storing data on computer systems, consideration has to be given to factors affecting file size and the quality of the stored data.
   a. Discuss the relationship between image quality and file size.
   b. Describe how an image file size may be reduced to enable it to be used in a web page.
   c. Describe how a text file size may be minimised, whilst the file still maintains its data quality.

2 Communications and the Internet

This page summarises what you will learn about computer communications. Tick the boxes on this page when you are confident you have learned each item.

2.1 Data transmission

TICK THE BOX WHEN YOU HAVE LEARNED:

- [ ] the different methods of data transmission
- [ ] the meaning of simplex and duplex transmission
- [ ] the meaning and uses of serial and parallel transmission
- [ ] what a USB connection is
- [ ] what causes transmission errors
- [ ] error-check procedures including parity checks
- [ ] the purpose and use of check digits and checksums.

2.2 The Internet

TICK THE BOX WHEN YOU HAVE LEARNED:

- [ ] what the Internet is
- [ ] what the World Wide Web is
- [ ] what HTML is used for
- [ ] what a protocol is
- [ ] the protocols HTTP and HTTPS
- [ ] what encryption and authentication are
- [ ] the protocols TCP and IP
- [ ] how IP address and URL are used to identify a website.

2.3 Online safety

TICK THE BOX WHEN YOU HAVE LEARNED:

- [ ] the main risks of Internet use
- [ ] how to protect yourself online
- [ ] the different types of malware and their effects
- [ ] software that is available to protect against malware and other risks.

2.1 Data transmission

How data is transmitted

Data is transmitted between computers as binary (on/off) signals. There are a number of different transmission media. Each type of transmission has advantages and suitable uses.

Fact check

Data transmission: Many modern uses of computers depend on data transmission (e.g. the Internet, networks, emails). Data is transmitted between devices as a stream of on/off signals. Data can be transmitted through cables or wireless (such as radio signals).

Main types of cable:

- **Twisted pair:** Two thin copper wires are twisted together. The signals are sent as electricity.
- **Coaxial:** This is a thicker metal cable protected by a layer of insulation. The signals are sent as electricity.
- **Fibre-optic:** This is a cable made of strands of transparent plastic wound together. Fibre-optic cable transmits signals as pulses of light.

These are the advantages and disadvantages of the different types of cable:

- Twisted pair – the advantages are that it is the least expensive option, it is made of flexible wire and is easy to install. The disadvantages are that twisted pair cable can be affected by electrical interference and it is not suitable for long-distance transmission.
- Coaxial cable – this is a metal cable, surrounded by a layer of insulation then another layer of metal. The advantage of this type of cable is that it resists electrical interference. The disadvantages are that coaxial cable is more expensive than twisted pair cable and is not as flexible.
- Fibre-optic cable – this is the most modern type of cable. Its advantage is that it is unaffected by electrical interference. Fibre-optic cable is a good choice for long-distance cable links. Its disadvantage is that it is somewhat expensive.

Check your readiness

Produce a table showing the different types of transmission media, with their advantages, disadvantages and main uses. List key terms with their definitions. Find images of all main transmission media.

Key terms

Long-distance transmission: when a computer sends a signal to another computer

Short-distance transmission: when the different parts of a single computer send signals to each other.

Key terms

Transmission medium: the system that carries signals

Simplex communications: communications that go one way only (e.g. when listening to the radio)

Duplex communications: communications that go both ways (e.g. when talking on the phone)

Half-duplex communications: communications that go both ways, but each side has to take turns (e.g. when using a walkie-talkie system)

Serial or parallel?

Transmission may be serial or parallel. In serial transmission bits are sent one at a time. In parallel transmission bits are sent in sets of eight, via eight different wires. Each method has advantages and disadvantages. Parallel transmission is used to speed up the inner working of the computer.

You need to know:
- the difference between serial and parallel transmission
- the comparative advantages and disadvantages of the two types of transmission.

Fact check

Data transmission: Data is transmitted in groups of eight bits (one byte).

Serial transmission: The eight bits are sent one after the other. Wireless transmission is always serial. Serial transmission is used for long-distance connections (e.g. when using the Internet).

Parallel transmission: The eight bits are sent down eight different wires. They all arrive at the same time. Parallel transmission is used for short-distance communications, for example to connect different parts of the same computer.

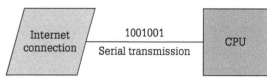

Serial transmission – the eight bits are sent one after the other down the same wire

These are the advantage and disadvantage of serial transmission:

- The advantage is that serial transmission is more reliable than parallel transmission, particularly over long distances.
- The disadvantage is that serial transmission is slightly slower than parallel transmission.

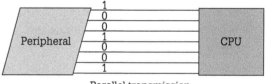

Parallel transmission – the eight bits are sent at the same time along different wires

These are the advantages and disadvantages of parallel transmission:

- The advantage is that parallel communication is quicker, because all eight bits are transmitted in one go.
- The disadvantage is that there is greater risk of error than with serial transmission. The processing required is more complex. The cables are wider.

Uses of serial and parallel transmission: Serial transmission is used for long-distance communication. The reliability of these connections is important. Parallel transmission is used for very short links, between the different parts of a computer. The speed of these connections makes a significant difference to the speed of the computer. For medium distance links (e.g. from a computer to a printer) either method may be used.

Check your readiness

Without referring to your notes or this page, describe the two main types of transmission. List the advantages and disadvantages of each. Give the reasons for selecting different types of transmission for different purposes.

Data bus

Connections within the processor are called buses. Parallel transmission is used for these. Connections between the processor and peripherals are also called buses. Serial transmission is typically used for these links.

You need to know:
- how a data bus is used to connect the parts of a computer
- what the USB standard is.

Fact check

What is a data bus? A data bus is a short distance connection that transmits data inside the computer. A data bus can be serial or parallel.

Connecting processors: An integrated circuit (IC) is a collection of microscopic electronic circuits. Many of the ICs are stuck onto a board called a motherboard. The ICs are connected by parallel data buses.

Parallel data bus: A parallel bus is used to connect the parts of the processor. Parallel transmission is fast, so it makes the computer work fast.

Connecting peripherals: Peripherals are the devices connected to the computer (e.g. the mouse, keyboard and screen). Peripherals must be connected to the central processor of the computer. The final connection to the processor uses a data bus.

Serial data bus: Peripherals work much slower than the processor, so speed of connection is less important. A serial bus is used to connect peripherals to the processor.

USB: This is a common standard for connecting peripherals. The USB port is a socket where a USB cable can be plugged in. USB is a standard used all over the world by different manufacturers. Devices from many different manufacturers can be plugged in to the same port.

Key terms

USB: universal serial bus

In USB:

universal: a common standard

serial: uses serial transmission

bus: transmits data inside the computer.

Check your readiness

Explain when you would use a serial or parallel data bus and give reasons for your answer. Look for images of the USB port and connector.

Transmission errors

Every data transmission includes the risk of errors. For this reason transmission methods include double-checks to ensure that data is received correctly. If there is a problem, the data must be sent again until it is correct.

You need to know:
- what transmission errors are
- the different types of error
- the stages of the ARQ process.

Fact check

Transmission errors: Sometimes data isn't transmitted correctly. Transmission errors can have serious effects, because the data will be wrong. To reduce errors we put systems in place to check data for errors when it is transmitted, detect any errors and correct them.

Causes of errors include: mistakes in preparing the data (e.g. typing mistakes); failures of equipment or transmission medium; and external interference interrupting the transmission.

Possible errors: Bits might be lost from the data stream. Extra bits might be added to the data stream. Bits might change value from 1 to 0. Two bits might swap around (which is a transposition error).

ARQ: This is a method to ensure correct transmission of data. The transmitter sends a packet of data. When the receiver gets the data packet, it checks for errors. If the receiver finds no errors, it will send an acknowledgement. If the transmitter doesn't receive an acknowledgement, it has to send the data again.

Time out: The transmitter will keep sending the data until it receives an acknowledgement. Eventually the transmitter stops trying. This is called time out.

Check your readiness

Without looking at your notes or this page, list the types and causes of transmission error. Draw a diagram of the ARQ process. Write the definitions of the key terms.

Key terms

Transcription error: an error when copying data from one form to another (e.g. when typing it in)

Transposition error: two data items swap position

Transmitter: the device that sends the data

Receiver: the device that receives the data

ARQ: stands for "Automatic Repeat ReQuest".

Parity check

It is important to spot errors in transmission. An even parity bit is an extra bit added to a byte. After the parity bit has been added, every byte should have an even number of 1s in it. If a byte is received with an odd number of 1s, then an error has occurred. This is called an even parity check. An odd parity check is sometimes used instead of an even parity check. With an odd parity check, the number of 1s should be an odd number.

You need to know:
- what parity bits are
- how to use parity bits to detect errors.

Key term

Parity: description of a number as even or odd.

Fact check

Use of parity checks: Parity checks are used to spot errors in data. A parity check cannot correct the errors. If the check spots an error, the receiver can ask for a repeat transmission.

Parity bit: An even parity bit is an extra bit added to a byte of data. If the number of 1s is odd then add an extra 1. If the number of 1s is even then add a 0. Now every byte of data has an even number of 1s. The parity bit can be included in the byte or a separate transmission.

What the transmitter does: The transmitter counts how many 1s there are in each byte it sends. The transmitter adds a parity bit before sending it. Now every byte has an even number of 1s.

What the receiver does: The receiver counts how many 1s in each byte it receives. If it is an even number, it sends an acknowledgement. If it is an odd number, there has been an error.

Errors the parity bit method will spot: It will spot when a bit has been lost from the signal, and when a bit has changed value. In these cases the number of bits will turn from even to odd.

Errors the parity bit method will not spot: It will not spot when two bits have been lost, and when two bits have swapped position. In these cases the number of bits stays even.

Odd parity: Some computer systems use odd parity instead of even parity. Odd parity works exactly the same as even parity but every byte must have an ODD number of 1s. Of course both computers must agree which parity system is in use before transmission.

Check your readiness

Work alone or with another student. Pick a number between 1 and 255. Convert it to binary. Send it to another student along with an even parity bit. That student will check for errors and convert back to denary. Try including deliberate errors in the transmission. Will your partner spot them?

Check digit and checksum

Other methods of detecting errors are check digits and checksums. Like a parity bit, these are calculated separately by receiver and transmitter. The two versions should match. Check digits and checksums may be calculated from either denary or binary values.

You need to know:
- what check digits and checksums are
- how to calculate check digits and checksums
- when to use check digits and checksums.

Fact check

Check digit: A check digit is a single digit added to the end of a transmitted number. It is used to check for errors. It is worked out from the denary values that are transmitted. There is more than one way to work out a check digit.

Checksum: A checksum is a number added to the end of a transmitted series of numbers. It is worked out by adding the numbers together or it may be calculated by adding together the 1s in a binary transmission.

Transmitter and receiver: The transmitter and receiver work out what the check digit or checksum should be. Both computers should get the same result. If they get different results, it shows a transmission error has occurred.

Simple check digit: Add up all the digits in the number. Divide by 10 and find the remainder (mod 10). The remainder is the check digit. Some check digits use mod 11.

Problems with the simple check digit: This type of check digit cannot identify a transposition error. Transposition is when two digits get swapped around. The transposition of two digits will not change the overall sum of the digits. More complicated methods have been invented to identify transposition errors.

Key terms
Modulo (or "mod"): the remainder after a division

Sum: the total from adding a series of numbers together.

Extension

Other check digit methods include The Luhn Method and the ISBN-10 method. Research these methods.

Check your readiness

Prepare a set of numbers for transmission. Calculate simple check digits and a checksum. Swap your results with another student and compare your checks.

2.1 Knowledge test

1. What are the main types of cable used in data transmission?

2. Give the advantages and disadvantages of the three main types of cable.

3. What is the alternative to cable as a means of data transmission?

4. Explain the difference between serial and parallel transmission.

5. When is it most appropriate to use serial transmission and why?

6. When is it most appropriate to use parallel transmission and why?

7. What is meant by "USB" and when is it used?

8. Explain the actions of the transmitter and receiver in the ARQ process.

9. You receive the following three-byte transmission. Each byte includes an even parity bit. Which of the bytes has an error in it?

    1 0 1 1 1 0 0 1

    0 0 1 1 1 0 0 1

    1 1 1 1 0 0 0 0

10. You receive the following three-number transmission. The final digit of each number is a simple check digit calculated using mod 10. Recalculate the check digit for each number to find which one has an error in it.

    8409981 - 9

    7845232 - 1

    6654914 - 0

11. What are the limitations of the simple check digit method?

12. You need to send the following three-number transmission. Calculate a checksum to be sent following this transmission.

    8409981

    7845232

    6654914

2.2 The Internet

What is the Internet?

The Internet is a huge network that connects computers all over the world. To use the Internet the correct software and protocols must be in place. Internet use is provided by a company called an Internet Service Provider (ISP).

You need to know:
- what the Internet is
- what you need to make an Internet connection
- what services are offered by an Internet Service Provider (ISP).

Fact check

The Internet: This is a system of communication links. If your computer is connected to the Internet it can communicate with computers all over the world.

How big is the Internet? About half the people on Earth have used the Internet. Billions of computers and other devices are connected to the Internet.

How reliable is the Internet? Nobody is in charge of the Internet. It is the source of very good content, and also dangerous and harmful content. You must use the Internet with care.

What do you need in order to connect?
- Data transmission medium: cable or wireless connection.
- Internet software: software converts data on your computer into signals so it can be transmitted. It also converts signals from the Internet so you can read them.
- Shared protocols: protocols are standard rules about how data is turned into signals. All computers that connect to the Internet use the same protocols. Key protocols of the Internet are TCP and IP.

ISP: This is an organisation that helps you connect to the Internet. An ISP sends signals between the Internet and your computer; provides email (in most cases); and hosts a web page if you want one.

Check your readiness

Write a checklist of the things that need to be in place to make an Internet connection. Note the job of an ISP. Reflect in more depth on the opportunities and risks of the Internet in the modern world.

What is the World Wide Web?

The World Wide Web is made up of all the web pages in the world. A web page is a document that can contain multimedia content. It is read by a web browser, which shows it on the screen of your computer.

You need to know:
- what the World Wide Web is and why it is different from the Internet
- what a web page is
- how to use a web browser.

Fact check

Web page: A web page is a multimedia document that you can read over the Internet. Web pages can be viewed by software called a web browser. Web pages can include links to other web pages.

Web server: This is a computer that is permanently connected to the Internet. A website is a collection of web pages stored on a web server. This is called hosting the website. Your computer can make an Internet link to a web server, and get a copy of one or more web pages.

Web browser: This is the software that lets you look at web pages. A web browser gets the content of the web page. It displays the web page on your screen. It takes any inputs you type and sends them back to the web page.

How do you tell the browser which web page to show? Every web page has its own address. Type the address of the page in the browser or click on a hyperlink.

Check your readiness

Make sure you know the differences between a web page, a website, a web server and a web browser.

Key terms

The World Wide Web: the collection of all the web pages in the world. It is the most popular service available over the Internet

Multimedia: content that can include text, images, sound and video.

HTML

A web page is a document. Instructions have been added to the document using a language called HTML. HTML controls called tags change the way the document is displayed. HTML adds multimedia content and links to the document.

You need to know:
- what HTML means
- what HTML tags are
- how HTML sets the structure and appearance of a website.

Fact check

HTML: This stands for "hypertext markup language". HTML is the language used to make web pages. A web page consists of the text content of the page plus HTML controls (called tags). The HTML tags set the appearance and behaviour of the page on your screen. When you look at a web page in a browser you will not see the tags.

Tags: HTML tags are typed inside angular brackets < >. Tags usually come in pairs. The first tag turns a feature on, the next tag turns it off. For example these tags make "My family" into a page header.

<H1>My family</H1>

HTML tags control the structure and appearance of a web page.

Structure: Some HTML tags control the layout and structure of a web page. You can use HTML to add headings and sections. You can use HTML to add images and other multimedia content.

Appearance: Some HTML tags control the style and appearance of a web page, such as the colour and size of text. The example below determines the colours for a whole web page.

```
body {background-color:yellow;}
h1 {color:red;}
p {color:green;}
```

Key term

Hypertext: a text string that makes a link to a new web page. Most web pages include hypertext. When you click on a hypertext link your web browser will connect to the linked page. The new page will appear in your browser.

- Information about presentation may be stored in a file called a Cascading Style Sheet (CSS). The CSS is linked to the HTML file.
- Storing the presentation information in a separate file means it is easy to alter the appearance of the whole web site with a simple change.

Check your readiness

Define the meaning of hypertext and markup. Explain the difference between tags that affect structure, and tags that affect appearance.

HTTP: Hypertext transfer protocol

HTTP is a shared standard for communication. It is used to define links between web pages using a standard format. A variation called HTTPS adds extra features of authentication and encryption to increase security of data transfer.

You need to know:
- what HTTP and HTTPS are
- how authentication and encryption are used for security
- how cookies affect your use of the Internet.

Fact check

HTTP: This stands for "hypertext transfer protocol". HTTP is the protocol that makes hyperlinks work. Without HTTP the World Wide Web would not work. The address of every web page begins http:// or https://. That shows you that the page uses the HTTP protocol.

HTTPS: This stands for "HTTP secure". HTTPS is an extended protocol. HTTPS has extra features that are not part of the basic HTTP protocol. These features are authentication and encryption.

Authentication: Some websites are fake. Criminals have set them up to trick you into giving away your personal details or money. "Authentic" means not fake. Authenticating a website means checking that it is not fake.

Encryption: This is the process of disguising data so as to hide its content. HTTPS encrypts the data you send to a website. Only the company who made the website can read your details.

Cookies: When you use a website, it collects key data about what you do there. This data is packaged up as a small file called a cookie. The cookie is stored on your own computer. When you go back to the website, the cookie tells the website key facts about you, for example what you bought or looked at last time.

Key terms

Markup: a markup language adds controls to a text document. The controls do not appear as text. Some controls change the way the document appears. Some controls add features to the document.

A **protocol:** a shared standard for communication. If two computers use the same protocols they can share data.

Check your readiness

Without looking at your notes or this page, define the meaning of HTTP and HTTPS. Note the main differences between the two protocols. How do you know which protocol a website uses?

TCP/IP

The Internet uses a common protocol system called TCP/IP. Every web page can be identified using an IP address or a URL.

Fact check

Internet protocols: The protocol system called TCP/IP makes the Internet work:

- **TCP** stands for "Transmission Control Protocol". It controls the way data packets are transmitted on the Internet.
- **IP** stands for "Internet Protocol". This protocol makes sure the data packets go to the right place. Every location on the Internet has an IP address. IP sends the data to the right address.

IP address: Every device that is connected to the Internet has its own IP address. IP addresses are large binary numbers: they have 128 bits. IP addresses are stored in a directory called the Domain Name System (DNS).

URL (uniform resource locator): A URL is an alternative to the IP address. It is made of words instead of numbers. That makes it easier to read, type and remember. The URL has these three parts: protocol (http or https), domain name and path.

Domain name: The domain name identifies the server. Domain names often end with a short text code such as .com. This code is the top-level domain. It might identify the type of organisation or the country where the server is based.

Path: The domain name is often followed by a path. The path takes you to a single page on the website. A slash (/) is used to separate the path from the domain name.

MAC address: MAC stands for "media access control". It is a long binary number (like an IP address). It identifies a single device on a local area network (LAN).

Check your readiness

Without looking at your notes or this page, define the terms TCP and IP. Explain the difference between IP address and URL. Look at the URL of any website and identify the top-level domain, the domain name and the path.

2.2 Knowledge test

1. What needs to be in place to make an Internet connection?

2. Describe the job of an ISP.

3. Explain the meaning of the terms "web page", "website" and "web server".

4. What is the job of a web browser?

5. What is hypertext?

6. HTML is a markup language. What is markup?

7. HTML tags typically come in pairs. Why is that?

8. What is HTTP and what is it for?

9. What is the difference between HTTP and HTTPS?

10. Give the meaning of TCP and IP.

11. What is the difference between IP address and URL?

12. Here is an example of a website address: http://global.oup.com/about. Identify the top-level domain, the domain name and the path.

2.3 Safety online

Staying safe

There are risks to using the Internet. By using passwords we can protect our personal details. By behaving responsibly we can protect ourselves from harm. Be aware that there are dishonest people online.

Fact check

Passwords: You often have to enter personal details online. Personal details are often password protected. The password protects your details. Typing the right password confirms your identity.

Password quality: Use high-quality passwords; that is, passwords that are hard to guess. Do not use common words. Do not tell anyone else your password.

Watch out for tricks: Most people on the Internet behave honestly, but there are some people with bad intentions. Some adults pretend to be young people. Some criminals try to get your money. Remember these key points:

- Never give out personal details to people on the Internet.
- Never send money to a stranger.
- Never agree to meet someone on your own.

The Internet can save content: Be careful about what you write online. Some websites keep the things you write in public view for years. Teachers, parents and the police can see online content.

Dealing with bullies: Some people say hurtful things online. Don't accept their opinions. Block the contact. Tell someone you trust.

Behave responsibly: Don't be the source of problems on the Internet. Behave in a responsible way. Make the most of the opportunity to communicate with a wide range of people.

> **Check your readiness**
> Make notes on responsible use of the Internet. Keep to your own personal standards in everything you do online.

Malware and hacking

Malware is a general term for malicious software that can harm your computer and your data. There are various types of malware. You should know the meaning of the different key terms defined on this page.

Fact check

Some actions that will increase the risk of getting malware on your computer are:

- downloading free content from the Internet

- opening files attached to emails
- using storage devices sold by unreliable people.

These are types of malware that have special effects on your computer:

- Rootkit: This is malware that changes your operating system.
- Backdoor: This is malware that switches off security software to let other malware onto your computer.
- Spyware: This is a special kind of malware. Spyware is used by criminals and records your key presses. Spyware sends information about the keys you press to the owner of the spyware. The owners of the spyware can analyse the key press data to find out your passwords and other personal details.

Hacking: This involves accessing somebody else's computer without permission. Hackers usually work from a distance, using communications links. Hackers sometimes deliberately put malware on your computer to help them break into your system.

Check your readiness

List and define the different types of malware. What can you do to avoid getting malware on your computer?

Protective software

Anti-virus software protects a computer from malware. An Internet filter blocks connections to harmful sites. A firewall will screen all content passing in or out of a computer system. All of these are types of protective software.

Fact check

Anti-virus software: This is designed to identify and remove malware from your computer. It will screen incoming data and warn you about risky websites. Anti-virus software must be kept up to date, because new malware is being invented all the time.

Spam: This is unwanted email sent out to millions of people automatically. It is sometimes advertising for a product. Sometimes it is part of a criminal trick. Anti-virus software will often block spam.

Internet filter: This is software that blocks contact with unsuitable websites. It is sometimes called a net nanny or parental control software. Filters may also be installed in companies to control employees' use of the Internet.

Firewall: A firewall is made of hardware or software or both. A firewall screens all data passing in or out of a network. It traps every packet of data coming from the Internet. It checks the data using programmed rules. The firewall can prevent viruses getting on to the network, or block access to particular web sites.

A firewall can also be used to monitor and record all use of the Internet. It may alert users if their software tries to access the Internet (for example, for automatic updates).

Key terms

Malware: short for "malicious software". This is software made on purpose to do harm: it can destroy data and programs.

Types of malware:

Virus: malware that hides inside another file. The virus will make copies of itself. The copies will spread to other files on your computer and to other computers from yours.

Worm: malware in its own file, which copies itself to other computers across a network.

Trojan: malware disguised as a good file, such as a computer game or an image.

You need to know:

- how anti-virus software protects you against malware
- what protective software is available and what it does.

2.3 Knowledge test

1. If someone you meet online asks to meet up, what should you do?

2. Who should you tell about your Internet passwords?

3. Give the names of three different types of malware and explain the differences between them.

4. State three things you can do to avoid getting malware on your computer.

5. How does anti-virus software protect your computer from viruses?

6. What is a firewall?

Exam preparation

1. Use the information contained in topics 2.1 and 2.2 to describe the following terms:
   a. Simplex
   b. Duplex
   c. HTML
   d. HTTP

Exam-style questions

1. a. Explain the difference between serial transmission and parallel transmission.
   b. Give **one** advantage, **one** disadvantage and **one** example of the use of parallel transmission.
   c. Give **one** advantage, **one** disadvantage and **one** example of the use of serial transmission.
   d. The following bytes are to be transmitted using even parity. Complete the parity bits.

   Parity

	1	1	0	0	0	1	1

	0	0	0	0	0	1	0

	1	0	1	0	1	0	1

2. a. Name **three** examples of malware.
   b. For each example of malware named in part **a** state
      i   a feature of this malware
      ii an effect it can have on your computer or data
      iii a method to protect against it (all three methods must be different).
   c. Explain the purpose of a firewall.

3 The processor

This page summarises what you will learn about electronic processing. Tick the boxes on this page when you are confident you have learned each item.

3.1 Logic gates

TICK WHEN YOU HAVE LEARNED:

- [ ] what logic gates are
- [ ] the relationship between the input and output of a logic gate
- [ ] the symbol and truth table for a NOT gate
- [ ] the symbol and truth table for an AND gate
- [ ] the symbol and truth table for an OR gate
- [ ] the symbol and truth table for a XOR gate
- [ ] the symbol and truth table for a NAND gate
- [ ] the symbol and truth table for a NOR gate.

3.2 Logical processing

TICK WHEN YOU HAVE LEARNED:

- [ ] what logical deduction from premises is
- [ ] how to simplify logic statements using letters to stand for premises
- [ ] how to represent complex statements as logic circuits
- [ ] how to draw truth tables to match logic circuits with two inputs
- [ ] how to draw truth tables to match logic circuits with three or more inputs
- [ ] how to draw truth tables to match logic circuits where an input is passed to more than one logic gate
- [ ] how to use truth tables to solve logical problems.

3.3 Inside the CPU

TICK WHEN YOU HAVE LEARNED:

- [ ] the structure of the processor
- [ ] the job of the memory unit, CPU, control unit and ALU
- [ ] the stages of the fetch-execute cycle
- [ ] what happens at each stage of the fetch-execute cycle.
- [ ] the stored program model
- [ ] the four main registers and their jobs in the fetch-execute cycle.

3.1 Logic gates

Electronic processing

Logic gates are collections of electronic switches that change the flow of electricity. Electricity flows into the logic gate, and an electrical signal flows out. Logic gates can be joined together to make logic circuits.

Fact check

Electronic devices: Electronic devices contain electric switches. The electricity from one switch can turn another switch on or off. The flow of electricity is always changing, as switches turn on and off. This is how the processor works.

Computer processor: This holds data as on/off signals. It changes the electronic signals using logical steps.

On/off signals: We can describe the effect of the on/off switches on the electrical circuit as:

- on and off
- high and low voltage
- 1 and 0
- True and False.

Logic gates: Electronic switches are combined to form logic gates. Every logic gate has an input and an output. Some logic gates have one input, some have two inputs. Logic gates always have just one output. Different logic gates change the input to output in different ways.

Logic circuits: Logic gates can be joined together with wire connections to make logic circuits. Logic circuits can have many different inputs. Like logic gates, they have only one output. Different logic circuits change inputs to outputs in many different ways.

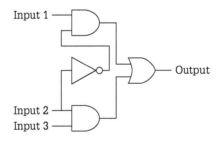

This logic circuit has three inputs and one output

Check your readiness

Define a logic gate and a logic circuit. What is the difference between the input and the output of a logic gate?

The NOT gate

A NOT gate is a simple logic gate that reverses an electrical signal. This gate has a symbol. A truth table shows how it changes input to output.

Fact check

Action of the NOT gate: The NOT gate has one input and one output. The NOT gate changes the input into its opposite:

- If the input is 1 (True), the output will be 0 (False).
- If the input is 0 (False), the output will be 1 (True).

The NOT gate works like putting the word "not" in a sentence. It changes the meaning of a sentence to its opposite. In logical terms, it changes "True" into "False".

Symbol: Each type of logic gate has a different symbol. This is the symbol for the NOT gate:

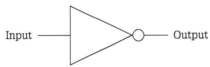

The NOT gate has one input and one output.

Truth table: We can show the two states of the NOT gate using a truth table.

Input	Output
True	False
False	True

Each row of the table shows one possible "state" for the NOT gate.

We generally draw a truth table using 1 and 0. This takes up less space.

Input	Output
1	0
0	1

> **Check your readiness**
>
> Without looking at your notes, draw the symbol for the NOT gate.
> Draw the truth table for the NOT gate.

The AND gate

> An AND gate is a simple logic gate that takes two inputs and produces one output. The output is False unless both inputs are True. This gate has a symbol. A truth table shows how it changes input to output.

Fact check

The AND gate has two inputs. The two inputs are independent (that means they don't affect each other).

You need to know:
- how to draw the symbol for a NOT gate
- how a NOT gate changes input to output
- the truth table for a NOT gate.

You need to know:
- how to draw the symbol for an AND gate
- how an AND gate changes input to output
- the truth table for an AND gate.

If both inputs are 1 (True), the output is 1 (True).

If either or both of the inputs is 0 (False), the output is 0 (False).

The AND gate is a bit like the word "and" in a sentence. If both halves of the sentence are true, then the whole sentence is true.

This is the symbol for the AND gate:

We usually call the two inputs A and B. Each input can be 1 (True) or 0 (False). That means the AND gate can be in four different states. This truth table shows the four states of the AND gate. The four states are the same as the first four binary numbers.

All the logic gates except the NOT gate have two inputs. The truth table of each of these logic gate starts like this:

A	B	Output
0	0	
0	1	
1	0	
1	1	

The output is different for each logic gate. The output of an AND gate is 1 if both A and B are 1. Here is the completed table:

A	B	A AND B
0	0	0
0	1	0
1	0	0
1	1	1

Check your readiness

Without looking at your notes or this page, draw the symbol for the AND gate. Draw the truth table for the AND gate.

The OR and XOR gates

The OR and XOR gates take two inputs and produce one output. The output of OR is 1 (True) if either input is 1 (True). The output of XOR is 1 (True) if the two inputs are different.

Fact check

The OR gate has two inputs. The inputs can be 1 (True) or 0 (False). If either or both of the inputs is 1 then the output is 1. If both inputs are 0 then the output is 0.

You need to know:

- the symbols for the OR and XOR gates
- how the OR and XOR gates change input to output
- the truth tables for the OR and XOR gates.

The OR gate is a bit like the word "or" in a sentence. This sentence is true if either half is true.

This is the symbol for the OR gate:

This is the truth table for the OR gate:

A	B	A OR B
0	0	0
0	1	1
1	0	1
1	1	1

XOR stands for "Exclusive OR". Another name for this gate is EOR. The XOR gate has two inputs.

If the inputs are the same then the output is 0.

If the inputs are different then the output is 1.

This is the symbol of the XOR gate. It looks like the OR gate with an extra line at the front.

This is the truth table for the XOR gate:

A	B	A XOR B
0	0	0
0	1	1
1	0	1
1	1	0

Check your readiness

Without looking at your notes or this page, draw the symbols for the OR and XOR gates. Draw the truth tables for the OR and XOR gates.

The NAND and NOR gates

The NAND and NOR gates take two inputs and produce one output. The output of NAND is true if both inputs are true. The output of NOR is true if the two inputs are different.

Fact check

The NAND gate is the opposite of an AND gate. The word NAND reminds you of this. It sounds like "not and". The output is 0 only if both inputs are 1.

You need to know:
- the symbols for the NAND and NOR gates
- how the NAND and NOR gates change input to output
- the truth tables for the NAND and NOR gates.

This is the symbol for the NAND gate. It looks like the AND gate with a circle next to it.

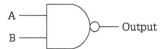

This is the truth table for the NAND gate. It is the opposite of an AND gate.

A	B	A NAND B
0	0	1
0	1	1
1	0	1
1	1	0

The NOR gate is the opposite of an OR gate. The word NOR reminds you of this. It sounds like 'NOT OR'. The output is on if both inputs are off.

The NOR gate looks like the OR gate with a circle next to it.

This is the truth table for the NOR gate. It is the opposite of an OR gate.

A	B	A NOR B
0	0	1
0	1	0
1	0	0
1	1	0

Check your readiness

Without looking at your notes or this page, draw the symbols for the NAND and NOR gates. Draw the truth tables for the NAND and NOR gates.

3.1 Knowledge test

1. Name each of the six logic gates you have learned about.

2. Draw the symbol for each gate next to its name.

3. Draw the truth table for each gate next to the symbol.

3.2 Logical processing

Logic statements

The logic of real-life statements matches up to the logic of the computer processor. That is why a computer can be used to help with real-life problems.

Fact check

Real-life logic: Logic is useful in real life. It helps us work out whether statements are true or false. This supports all types of decision making.

Composite statements: We can join statements together. We can join them with words such as "and", "or", "not". The result is called a composite statement.

Logical deduction: The truth of a composite statement depends on the truth of its premises. The laws of logic let us work out the truth of a conclusion from the truth of the premises.

Using the computer to solve problems: Inside the computer processor are logic gates, with names such as AND, OR, NOT. These gates can be matched up with real-life statements so that we can use computers to help with real-life problems.

Example: An alarm will be sounded if an oven is switched on AND the door is open. We can draw a truth table to see when the alarm would go off.

A (Door open)	B (Oven on)	Alarm (A AND B)
No	No	No
No	Yes	No
Yes	No	No
Yes	Yes	Yes

Check your readiness

You have developed understanding of this topic if you can see the underlying logical structure in real-life statements.

Simplify statements

We can use computers to solve real-life problems. Logic problems can be simplified into an abstract form. We use the letters A and B to stand for any two statements. Then we can use logic gates and truth tables to work out our conclusions.

You need to know:
- how logic allows us to work out whether statements are true.

Key terms

Logic statements: expressions that have a definite True or False value

Logical deduction: the process of using the laws of logic to work out whether statements are True or False

Premises: you know the truth value of premises at the start of a logical deduction

Conclusions: you can work out the truth of conclusions using the laws of logic.

You need to know:
- how to express logic statements in a simplified form
- how to draw truth tables to match composite logic statements.

Fact check

Applying logic to real life: Logic is about the structure and truth value of statements. The details of the logic statements do not matter. All that matters (from a logical point of view) is whether the statements are True or False.

Abstraction: Instead of using sentences we use letters, often A and B. This lets us concentrate on logic, and not worry too much about details.

Logical connectors: A and B stand for any logic statement. We can join A and B together using the six logical connectors you have already learned about:

- NOT
- AND
- OR
- XOR
- NAND
- NOR.

Truth tables: Each of these logical connectors matches the logic gates inside the processor. The rules for logic gates, truth tables and logical connectors all match exactly. Real-life logical rules and the workings of computers match up. This is because computers were made to help with logic and mathematics.

Example: A computer-controlled security system used this rule: to pass through security you must show an ID card OR use the fingerprint scanner.

Here is the truth table that matches this statement – it is only partially completed.

Show ID Card	Use fingerprint scanner	Allow to enter
No		
No		
Yes		
Yes		

Check your readiness

Complete the truth table shown above. Write it again using A and B instead of the detailed statements. Draw the logic gate that matches this table.

Logic circuits

Logic circuits are made of logic gates connected by wires. The electrical output of one gate becomes the input to the next gate. Logic circuits can match complex composite statements with many connectors.

You need to know:
- that logic gates are joined to form logic circuits
- how to make a logic circuit to match a composite logic statement.

Fact check

What is a logic circuit? Logic gates are electronic structures, inside the computer. Electricity goes into the gate, and electricity comes out. Logic gates can be wired together. The electricity coming out of one gate will go into the next gate. A series of logic gates wired together is called a logic circuit.

Drawing logic circuits: Draw the symbols for the logic gates. Draw a line to join the output of one gate to the input of the next gate.

Single logic gates match short statements: A single logic gate matches a statement with a single connector such as A or B. Pictured to the right is the gate that matches A OR B.

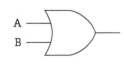

Logic circuits match long statements: A logic circuit with more than one gate matches a complex statement with more than one connector, for example (A AND B) OR C.

Start with the connections that are in brackets. Then add any further connections to make the complete circuit. Below is the circuit that matches (A OR B) AND (NOT C).

If there are no brackets in the statement, start with the first connector and join them in a simple series.

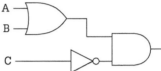

Check your readiness

Work alone or with another student. Write a composite logic statement with more than one connector. Draw a logic circuit to match this statement. Challenge the other student by giving them an example to match.

Truth tables and circuits

You can create a truth table to match a logic circuit by following four simple rules: label all inputs and outputs, create a table, fill in the inputs, and work out the outputs for each logic gate.

You need to know:
- how to make truth tables to match logic circuits.

Fact check

To make a truth table from a circuit follow these rules:
- Label every input and output in the circuit using letters.
- Draw a truth table with a column for every input and output.
- Fill in the inputs by counting up from 0 in binary.
- Fill in the outputs using the truth table rules for each logic gate in order.

Here is a simple logic circuit.
It represents the logical expression A NAND (NOT B).

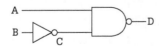

To complete a truth table for this circuit, follow these steps:

Step 1. In this circuit, the input and output to every logic gate is labelled with a letter. Draw a table to match the circuit. Include a column for each letter.

Step 2. Fill in the inputs using binary counting. There are two inputs, so the count goes from 0 0 to 1 1.

A	B	C	D
0	0		
0	1		
1	0		
1	1		

Step 3. Fill in the outputs for each gate. C is the output of a NOT gate. The input to the gate is B, so C is NOT B.

A	B	C = NOT B	D
0	0	1	
0	1	0	
1	0	1	
1	1	0	

D is the output of a NAND gate. The inputs to the gate are A and C, so D is A NAND C. The output is 1 unless both A and C are 1.

A	B	C = NOT B	D = A NAND C

Check your readiness

Draw the circuit changing the NAND gate to a NOR gate. Draw a truth table to match the new circuit.

0	0	1	1
0	1	0	1
1	0	1	0
1	1	0	1

The method for drawing a truth table to match a logic circuit will work with circuits that have more than two inputs. Just extend the binary counting to fill in 8, 16 or more rows of the table.

Fact check

Here is an example of a logic circuit. All inputs and outputs are labelled.

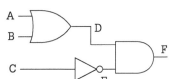

Draw a table with a column for every letter in the diagram. Fill in the inputs A, B and C using simple binary counting.

A	B	C	D	E	F
0	0	0			
0	0	1			
0	1	0			
0	1	1			
1	0	0			
1	0	1			
1	1	0			
1	1	1			

D, E and F are the outputs of the three logic gates. You know the inputs to these gates. Use the rules of the logic gates to work out the output in each case.

A	B	C	D = A OR B	E = NOT C	F = D AND E
0	0	0	0	1	0
0	0	1	0	0	0
0	1	0	1	1	1
0	1	1	1	0	0
1	0	0	1	1	1
1	0	1	1	0	0
1	1	0	1	1	1
1	1	1	1	0	0

Check your readiness

Draw a new version of the logic circuit shown on this page. Change the OR gate to a XOR gate. Change the AND gate to a NAND gate. Draw the truth table for the new circuit.

Solve a problem

You can make logic circuits to match logical expressions. You can make truth tables to match logic circuits. Combining these skills will allow you to solve logical problems.

You need to know:
- how to use logic circuits to solve logic problems.

Fact check

Logical deduction: A logical deduction starts with premises. Premises are statements that can be true or false. From the premises we can work out conclusions. The laws of logic will tell us whether the conclusions are true or false.

Using truth tables: A truth table will help us to work out whether conclusions are true or false. The truth table will show us what inputs lead to particular outputs.

Example 1: Here is the first truth table from *3.2 Truth tables and circuits*. It matches a logic circuit. A and B are the inputs. D is the final output of the circuit. What inputs produce a False output?

A	B	C = NOT B	D = A NAND C
0	0	1	1
0	1	0	1
1	0	1	0
1	1	0	1

There is only one row of the table with the output 0, so the answer to the question is that the output is false if A is True and B is False.

Example 2: Here is the second truth table from *3.2 Truth tables*. What is the output if this circuit when all three inputs are true?

A	B	C	D = A OR B	E = NOT C	F = D AND E
0	0	0	0	1	0
0	0	1	0	0	0
0	1	0	1	1	1
0	1	1	1	0	0
1	0	0	1	1	1
1	0	1	1	0	0
1	1	0	1	1	1
1	1	1	1	0	0

In the bottom row all three inputs are 1 (True). When all inputs are True, the output of the circuit is False.

> **Check your readiness**
>
> Look at the second table. If all inputs are False, what is the output? If A is True, and B and C are False, what is the output?

Repeat inputs

Logic circuits can use the same input in more than one logic gate. Draw a logic circuit with more than one wire from the inputs to the logic gates. Following the usual rules allows you to create a truth table to match the circuit.

You need to know:
- how to draw logic circuits and truth table where a single input is used in more than one logic gate.

Fact check

Repeated letters: In some logical expressions the same letter is used more than once, for example:

(A XOR B) AND (NOT B)

The letter B is used in two parts of the expression. When you draw the circuit the input B is wired into two gates.

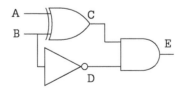

Draw the truth table using the methods you have learned. Fill in the two inputs, A and B.

A	B	C	D	E
0	0			
0	1			
1	0			
1	1			

Finally, calculate the output of each logic gate, using the rules of logic.

A	B	C (A XOR B)	D (NOT B)	E (C AND D)
0	0	0	1	0
0	1	1	0	0
1	0	1	1	1
1	1	0	0	0

The output is True if A is True and B is False.

Check your readiness

Draw a logic circuit for (NOT A) AND (A XOR B). Draw a truth table to match this circuit.

3.2 Knowledge test

Here is a logic statement: An alarm will sound if the door is opened AND the correct passcode is NOT entered.

1. Simplify this statement into an abstract structure.

2. Draw a logic circuit to match this statement.

3. Draw a truth table to match this statement.

4. When is the output of this statement true?

Here is a picture of a logic circuit.

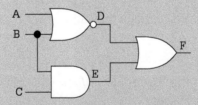

5. Write the logic statement that matches this circuit.

6. Draw a truth table to match this circuit.

7. What is the output of the following circuit if all inputs are false?

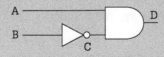

3.3 Inside the CPU

The central processing unit (CPU)

The processor consists of two parts – the main memory and the central processing unit (CPU). The CPU is made up of the arithmetic and logic unit (ALU) and the control unit. These different parts work together to transform data by altering electronic signals.

Fact check

The processor: Processing happens inside a part of the computer called the processor. Inside the processor, data is held as electronic signals. Data is altered by changes in electronic signals.

The processor has two parts, connected by data buses:

- main memory, where data is held
- the CPU, where data is altered.

Main memory: The main memory stores data and instructions in binary form. Main memory is divided into memory locations. Every memory location has a different address. The address of each location is a binary number.

The CPU: This is where data is processed. The CPU has two parts:

- The ALU: In the ALU the data is passed through logic circuits. The logic circuits change the electrical signals. They make changes using the rules of arithmetic and logic.
- Control unit: This controls all the other parts of the processor. It takes data and instructions from the main memory. It tells the ALU how to process the data. It sends the results back to main memory when processing is finished. It sends data to the peripherals. The control unit has a timer to make sure all the actions are carried out in order, one after the other.

Key term

Main memory: where data is held; also called random access memory (RAM) or immediate access store (IAS).

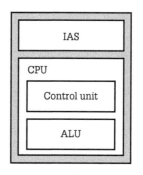

The structure of the processor

Check your readiness

Draw a diagram of the processor and its components. On the diagram note the function of each component.

The fetch-execute cycle

The computer uses a binary code called machine code to store instructions. The processor fetches machine code instructions from memory and executes them. This is called the fetch-execute cycle. Both instructions and data are stored in the electronic memory as binary numbers.

Fact check

Machine code instructions: The CPU gets instructions from main memory. Instructions are held in the main memory as binary numbers. Each number is a code that stands for a different computer action. The CPU decodes the number, then carries out the action.

Instruction set: Every CPU has a set of instructions that it knows. This is called the CPU's instruction set. Every instruction has a code number. A logic circuit in the CPU called the decoder turns the code number into the right instruction. Computers made by different companies can have different instruction sets.

The fetch-execute cycle: To use the instructions in main memory the CPU follows these actions:

1. Fetch – the control unit fetches a machine code instruction from the main memory.
2. Decode – the control unit decodes the instruction so it knows what action to carry out.
3. Execute – the control unit sends the instruction to the ALU. The ALU carries out the action.

FETCH
Instruction

DECODE
Instruction

EXECUTE
Instruction

Stored program model: The stored program model describes the basic working of the computer. Instructions and data are stored as electronic numbers in the main memory. The CPU fetches instructions and data from main memory. The CPU executes the instructions and this processes the data. The CPU sends any results back to main memory for storage.

Check your readiness

Without looking at this page, draw the fetch-execute cycle. Write notes on your diagram explaining what happens at each stage.

Registers and buses

The processor contains very small areas of memory called registers. They hold a very small amount of data but they offer very quick access. There are four important registers. Each has a different job in the fetch-execute cycle.

You need to know:
- what registers and buses are
- the function of the different registers and buses in the fetch-execute cycle.

Fact check

Register: A register is a very small area of memory. A register typically stores only one binary number. There are several registers inside the CPU. The CPU can access the data in the registers very quickly. The numbers in the registers are changing all the time the computer is working. The registers hold the instructions and data in use during one fetch-execute cycle.

Four registers are important in the fetch-execute cycle:

- The **program counter (PC)** holds the address of the next instruction to fetch.

- The **memory address register (MAR)** holds an address to read from or write to.
- The **instruction register (IR)** holds the instruction currently being executed.
- The **memory data register (MDR)** holds data just read from memory, or about to be written to memory.

Sequence and interrupts: Normally the PC counts through the memory locations one by one. Sometimes this sequence is interrupted, for example as follows:

- Program instructions might tell the PC to go to a new memory location.
- A signal from a peripheral can interrupt the computer's work.

Buses: The registers and other parts of the processor are connected by wires called buses. There are three types:

- An address bus transmits addresses.
- A data bus transmits data.
- A control bus transmits control signals (instructions).

Check your readiness

Give the names of the four registers. Summarise the job that each one does.

3.3 Knowledge test

1. The processor of the computer is divided into two parts: the main memory and the CPU. Describe the different jobs of the two parts.

2. How is each memory location identified?

3. The CPU is divided into two parts. What are their names?

4. Where are the logic circuits? What do logic circuits do?

5. Where is the timer? What is its job?

6. What is the name of the code that represents instructions as binary numbers?

7. What is an instruction set?

8. What happens at each stage of the fetch-execute cycle?

9. The stored program model describes the job of the main memory. What does the main memory do in this model?

10. Here are four important registers. What is the job of each register? The four are:
    a the program counter (PC)
    b the memory address register (MAR)
    c the instruction register (IR)
    d the memory data register (MDR).

Exam preparation

1. Use the information contained in topic 3.1 and draw the diagrams to represent the following logic gates:
   a   AND
   b   OR
   c   NOT
   d   XOR
   e   NAND
   f   NOR

Exam-style questions

1. a   Name the logic circuits that are combined to form a NAND gate.
    b   Draw the truth tables for the OR and XOR logic gates and explain the difference between the two.
    c   The following truth table represents a logic circuit with three inputs, A, B and C, and one output, Z. Draw the logic circuit to match the truth table.

A	B	C	X	Y	Z
0	0	0	0	1	1
0	0	1	0	0	0
0	1	0	0	1	1
0	1	1	0	0	0
1	0	0	0	1	1
1	0	1	0	0	0
1	1	0	1	1	0
1	1	1	1	0	1

2. a   Name the parts of the CPU that perform the following functions:
    i   store data before it is processed
    ii   transport data from one part of the CPU to another
    iii perform calculations in the CPU.
    b   Describe the three elements of the fetch-execute cycle.

4 Hardware

This page summarises what you will learn about hardware. Tick the boxes on this page when you are confident you have learned each item.

4.1 Input devices

TICK WHEN YOU HAVE LEARNED:

☐ how manual devices are used for data input

☐ the different types of touch screen

☐ how digital cameras and microphones work

☐ how barcodes are used

☐ the different types of scanners and their uses

☐ what conditions can be detected by sensors

☐ how feedback is used to maintain a control system.

4.2 Output devices

TICK WHEN YOU HAVE LEARNED:

☐ the different types of monitors and the technology they use

☐ the different types of printers and when to choose each type

☐ how sound output is produced and used

☐ what an actuator is and how actuators are used in industry

☐ how cutters and 3D printers are used to create objects

☐ the use of output in mobile technologies

☐ the use of output in modern manufacturing.

4.3 Memory and storage

TICK WHEN YOU HAVE LEARNED:

☐ the difference between primary storage and secondary storage

☐ the difference between RAM and ROM

☐ how to measure file size using bytes

☐ how to estimate the storage requirements of a data file

☐ how magnetic storage works and its uses

☐ how optical storage works and its uses

☐ what solid state storage is and how it is used

☐ how different types of storage are used in real life

☐ the right storage choices for different real-life needs.

4.1 Input devices

Keyboard and mouse

The keyboard and mouse are familiar and useful devices used for manual input. They convert text and positional data into binary signals.

Fact check

What is an input device? Data is held in the computer in digital form. When data is input to the computer it is converted to digital form. An input device is any piece of equipment that turns data into electronic signals that can be processed by the computer.

The keyboard: The keyboard is used for manual input of text data. When you press a key on the keyboard it is pushed down to make an electrical connection. That sends an electrical signal to the processor.

The mouse: The mouse is used for manual input of positional data. A mouse can sense its movement across a surface. It does this with a light and a small camera. The mouse sends data about its changing position to the computer.

Other devices

These other devices can be used to send positional data by hand to the computer:

- A trackball is used by people who find a mouse uncomfortable to use. You move the ball with your fingers and the device stays still.
- A touchpad is used when you don't want to plug any other devices into the laptop.
- A game console gives you control over a computer game.

Manual input

Advantages of mouse and keyboard are that they are:

- easy and familiar to use
- free with a typical computer
- useful for a wide range of tasks.

There are also disadvantages:

- Using a mouse and keyboard is slower than using automatic systems.
- Human users can make mistakes.
- People get tired if they type for a long time.

Check your readiness

Note the workings, uses, advantages and disadvantages of devices used for manual input.

You need to know:
- what an input device is
- how the mouse and keyboard work
- how input devices are used in computer systems.

Key terms

Manual input: data being entered by hand (by a human user)

Automatic input: data being read directly by the computer.

Touch screens

A touch screen is used for both input and output. The processor receives information about where the user has touched the screen. There are three different types of touch screen.

Touch screen: This has a double function. It is an output device that displays information for the user. It is a manual input device that lets the user make selections from the display, by touching the screen. The touch screen sends positional data to the processor.

There are three types of touch screen:

- resistive
- capacitive
- infra-red.

Resistive: A resistive screen has two thin layers that conduct electricity. When you touch the screen you push the two layers together. This sends an electrical signal matching the place where you pressed the screen. These are the advantages and the disadvantage of a resistive screen:

- Advantages are that this is the least expensive type of screen; also, you can touch the screen with any object and it will detect it.
- The disadvantage is that this type of screen is easily damaged.

Capacitive: A capacitive screen has a grid of conductive strips laid each side of the screen. If you touch the screen with your bare finger, you take some of the electrical charge from the screen. The screen checks which strip on either side has the changed charge: your finger is at the place where the two strips cross.

These are the advantages and the disadvantage of a capacitive screen:

- A capacitive screen is stronger than a resistive screen; also, it makes a brighter image.
- The disadvantage is that you must use your bare finger, not a pen or glove.

Infra-red: An infra-red touch screen has a grid of invisible beams projected across the screen. A finger, pen or pointer will break the beams. The screen checks which two beams have been broken by the pointer.

These are the advantages and the disadvantage of an infra-red screen:

- An infra-red screen has a strong bright image; also, you can touch the screen with any object.
- The disadvantage is that this type of screen is more expensive than other touch screens.

Check your readiness

Draw a table with information on the three types of touch screen, including the advantages and disadvantages of each.

Camera and microphone

Digital cameras and microphones turn images and sounds into electronic binary signals and input this data to the processor.

Fact check

Digital camera: This turns light into electronic signals. It has an aperture (a hole) at the front. The aperture contains a lens. Light comes through the aperture. The lens focuses the light onto a sensitive electronic surface. The surface is made of a grid of tiny sensors. The sensors inside the camera turn the pattern of light into electrical signals.

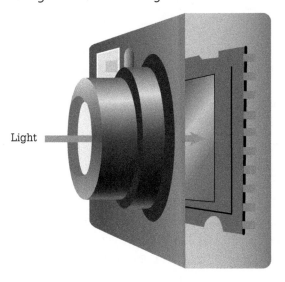

Digital microphone: This turns sound into electrical signals. Sound waves are movements of the air. A microphone detects the movement of the air. A microphone has a component that vibrates when hit by sound waves. Examples of these components are:

- a thin sheet with a coil of wire around a magnet
- a ribbon of metal foil with a magnet around it.

The vibration is converted to a digital signal.

Use in everyday life: Modern mobile phones have microphones and digital cameras. People use their phones to make recordings. Sometimes they record their ordinary lives. Sometimes dramatic and significant events are recorded by ordinary bystanders.

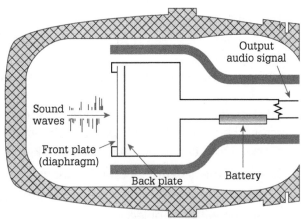

The microphone converts sound waves into an electrical signal

Check your readiness

Draw diagrams or write brief explanations of how digital cameras and microphones work. Look for stories in the news that include video and sound recordings made by ordinary people using their phones.

Barcode readers

Bar codes and QR codes store codes that identify objects. The codes are stored as patterns of black and white bars.

Fact check

Barcode: A barcode is a way of holding a code number. The number is turned into a pattern of black and white bars. Patterns of wide and narrow bars represent different digits.

Use of barcodes: Barcodes are printed on the wrappers and labels of products. Each product has a different code. When you buy the product the EPOS terminal reads the barcode. The EPOS terminal looks up product details using the code.

An EPOS terminal uses many different input and output devices

Barcode reader: A barcode reader flashes light onto the barcode. The light bounces back to the reader. Sensors in the reader can detect the pattern of light and dark from the barcode. The pattern of light and dark lines represents a code number. A barcode scanner is similar but it moves light across the barcode.

These are the advantages of using barcode readers:

- Using a barcode reader is quicker and more accurate than manual data entry.
- A barcode can be printed by any ordinary black and white printer.

There are also disadvantages:

- A barcode reader can only do one job – read barcodes.
- A barcode reader is not part of an ordinary computer; it must be bought separately.

QR code: This stands for "quick response" code. Businesses use QR codes to track products.

These are the advantages of QR codes:

- A QR code has a large pattern that stores more data than an ordinary barcode.
- A QR code can store a web link (e.g. in adverts).
- QR codes can be read by special devices, but can also be read using a smartphone app.

Barcode reader in action

> ### Check your readiness
> Note the uses, advantages and disadvantages of barcodes and QR codes.

A QR code can be read by a mobile phone

You need to know:
- how barcode readers are used to input data
- the use of barcodes and quick response (QR) codes in everyday life.

Key term
EPOS: stands for "electronic point of sale". An EPOS terminal is used at the checkout of many shops.

Scanners

A scanner records the image of an object. A 2D scanner records the surface of an object, such as a page. A 3D scanner records the solid object from all sides.

You need to know:
- how 2D and 3D scanners work
- what OCR and OMR readers do
- the advantages and disadvantages of different types of scanner.

Fact check

Document scanner: A document scanner scans a flat surface, such as a page, to record the content. The simplest form of scanner records the document as a single image.

OMR: This stands for "optical mark recognition". An OMR scanner detects marks made on paper or card, for example when someone makes a selection from a list by marking one item. The OMR scanner can detect which item is marked. This data is passed to the computer. OMR can be used to mark exams, analyse surveys and record results in voting systems. It can only record ready-made choices.

OCR: This stands for "optical character recognition". An OCR scanner takes an image of a document. Software linked to the scanner can detect the different letters in the document. OCR is used to turn paper documents into text stored on a computer. OCR scanning is much quicker than typing.

3D scanner: A 3D scanner records the whole shape of a solid object. Some 3D scanners use light, some use physical contact. All the information about the object is sent to the computer. Now the computer has a complete record of the object. It can make a 3D image on screen, or even a copy of the object.

Uses of 3D scanners include:

- industrial – to copy and manufacture objects
- medical – to scan parts of the body for diagnosis
- cultural – to record works of art.

Key term

Dimension: in 2D or 3D the "D" stands for "dimension". Dimension means a direction of movement or measurement.

Check your readiness

Note the different types of scanner and their uses.

Sensors

Sensors can detect environmental conditions and send this data to the processor in digital form. There are many types of sensor. Each can detect one feature of the environment.

You need to know:
- how sensors are used to input environmental conditions in digital form
- the use of sensors for a range of applications.

Fact check

Sensors: These are automatic input devices. A sensor measures and records the environment outside the computer. The measurement is converted to a digital value and inputted to the processor. Each type of sensor records just one feature of the environment:

- Light sensors tell the computer how dark or bright it is.
- Temperature sensors tell the computer how warm or cold it is.
- Magnetism is used to detect metal objects or to find a compass direction.
- Humidity is used where the presence of moisture is important, for example in agriculture and for dry storage.
- Acidity is important in science, cooking and industry.
- Motion can be detected – for example, computer games consoles can detect when they are moved around in the air.

Use of sensors: Computers use sensor data to monitor, record and even control the environment.

Robotics: Motion and pressure sensors are used in robotics. A robotic device that moves must have pressure sensors. Pressure sensors tell the robotic device if it touches an obstacle. Then the device can stop, move back or go around the obstacle.

Advantages of using sensors compared to a person making a record are as follows:

- Sensors are more accurate and precise.
- They can record constantly without a break.
- They can record data in places people cannot go.

These are the disadvantages of using sensors compared to a person making a record:

- Sensors can detect only one thing.
- Sensors and computer systems must use pre-set responses, they are not as flexible as people.

Check your readiness
List the main types of sensors and their uses.

Control systems

Control systems operate without a human user in charge. The computer monitors the effects of its own actions and adjusts its output to preserve a steady state.

You need to know:
- what control systems are
- how control systems are used in everyday life
- the advantages and disadvantages of control systems.

Fact check

What is a control system? This is an automatic system run by a computer. The computer monitors an environmental condition using sensors. The computer changes the environmental condition using devices it controls. Computers can control a wide range of devices such as motors, lights and heaters. The computer is given a target (e.g. a temperature or an end state) and will work to achieve or maintain that target.

Feedback: In a control system the input and output affect each other:

- The computer's actions cause output
- The computer measures its own output

- The computer uses this measurement as input
- The computer compares the input to the target state and adjusts its actions
- This changes the output and the cycle continues.

System

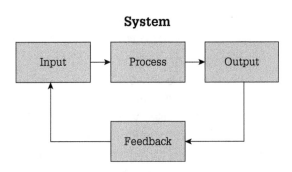

Advantages of using a computer to control a process are that a computer:

- never gets tired or bored
- can measure very accurately
- can go where people cannot go
- can react very quickly in an emergency.

There are some disadvantages:

- Using a computer to control a process can be expensive.
- If something unexpected happens, a human operator is needed.

Examples of control systems include:

- manufacture by robots in factories
- controlling household devices day and night
- aeroplane autopilot systems and other forms of transport control.

Check your readiness

Draw the feedback cycle. List examples of the use of feedback to control processes.

4.1 Knowledge test

1. What are the two main manual input devices used with ordinary desktop computers? What sort of data is input by each device?

2. What are the disadvantages of manual input devices?

3. What are the three types of touch screen?

4. Give the advantages and disadvantages of each of the three types of touch screen.

5. Explain the purpose of an aperture in the action of a digital camera.

6. A digital microphone has a component that vibrates. What is the purpose of this component?

7. What is the advantage of using barcodes over other forms of data input?

8. What is the difference between a barcode and a QR code?

9. Name three types of scanner and what data they send to the processor.

10. Name three types of sensor and what they can detect.

11. How does the feedback cycle enable the computer to work without a human operator?

4.2 Output devices

Monitors and display

A monitor creates an instant image that shows you the output from the computer system when it is in use.

Fact check

Monitor: This is the screen attached to a computer. It is also called a visual display unit (VDU). The monitor is an output device. It displays text, images and video. The monitor responds immediately to your actions, showing the result. The display is known as "soft copy" of data. If you want permanent output you must use a printer.

Two types of monitor are used on most modern computers:

• LCD (liquid crystal display) – the least expensive flat-screen option
• LED (light emitting diode) – a more expensive option, which can have a brighter picture.

LCD: Liquid crystal is a material that alters when electricity flows through it. The changes to the liquid crystal make it more or less transparent. The LCD screen has a backlight that shines through the liquid crystal layer. Sending different electrical signals to the display lets light through in different places, and this makes the display.

LED: An LED is like a small light bulb. LED bulbs use less electricity than ordinary bulbs, but they are more expensive to buy. LED bulbs can be used as the light source for an ordinary LCD screen. Other screens are made of millions of tiny "organic LEDs" (OLEDs) arranged in a grid to make a screen display. OLED displays are high quality but expensive.

Projectors: These are used to display computer images for a large group of people to look at. There are two common types:

• An LCD projector works as a beam of light passes through the LCD onto a screen.
• A digital light projector (DLP) uses light that bounces off a grid of thousands of tiny mirrors that can move. DLP is used in many cinemas. This is called digital cinema.

Check your readiness

List the different types of screen and projector and explain the technology used in each case.

Printers

A printer is needed if you want a permanent copy of your output. The two most common forms of printer are inkjet and laser printers. An inkjet printer is suitable for inexpensive quality printing. A laser printer is suitable for people who need to print a lot.

You need to know:
- what a printer is and how it is used
- the different types of printer
- the right printer for a particular use.

Fact check

Hard copy: Printed output is known as a "hard copy" of data. Hard copy provides a permanent record of the data. However, a printer takes longer than a monitor to show the output. Printed output takes up more space and is worse for the environment.

Inkjet printer: Electrical signals control jets that spray ink onto the page. This is the least expensive type of printer and produces high-quality images. However, an inkjet printer is not very fast, and ink refills can be very expensive. An inkjet printer may be suitable for home use or for a small business.

Laser printer: A laser printer uses fine black dust called toner. The laser printer contains a drum (a cylinder). The drum is coated with static electricity. The static electricity makes the toner stick to the drum. A laser beam removes static electricity to leave a pattern of toner. Many laser printers can print only in black and white, but colour printers are available.

Laser printers are usually larger, heavier and more expensive to buy than inkjet printers. However, they are generally much faster, and the cost per page is cheaper because toner is cheaper to refill than ink. A laser printer is a good choice if you need to do a lot of printing. For example, laser printers are often used in schools and in businesses.

Check your readiness
Make a list of the advantages and disadvantages of the two common types of printer.

Sound

Sound output is used in a different way to visual output. Speakers turn electrical signals from the computer into sounds.

You need to know:
- what a speaker is and how it works
- the advantages and disadvantages of different devices
- the best devices for different uses.

Fact check

Sound: Sound waves are vibrations in the air. All sound output comes from turning electronic signals from the computer into vibrations in the air.

Uses of sound output: Sound output does not leave a permanent record, but it has many uses. It can give you information when you cannot look at the screen. It can be used for warnings and alarms. We also enjoy listening to sounds such as music and stories.

Sound output devices: There are two main types – speakers and headphones. Headphones are just small speakers held very close to your ear.

How a speaker works: Most speakers contain a plastic or metal cone. The bottom of the cone is fixed to wire coiled around a magnet. Electrical signals make the magnet attract and repel the metal coil. The coil moves up and down, pulling and pushing the cone. The moving cone pumps sounds out into the air.

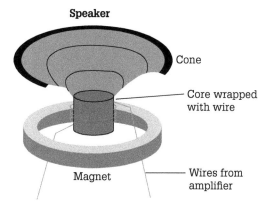

Speaker

Cone

Core wrapped with wire

Magnet

Wires from amplifier

A speaker turns electrical signals into sounds

Headphones: These allow people to listen to sounds without disturbing anyone else. As the speakers are close to your ears, the sound can be quiet but you can hear it clearly.

Choosing the right sound output: Most computers have built-in speakers. People who want better quality sound can buy better speakers and plug them into the computer. People who want to listen to sound privately can use headphones. Remember that loud music can harm your hearing and annoy other people, so be sensible about your use of sound output.

Check your readiness

Make notes on how sound output is generated by a speaker.

Actuators

Actuators are machines controlled by the computer. They can be used to move objects, or themselves, around. They can be used in automated systems (e.g. manufacturing processes).

You need to know:
- what an actuator is
- the different ways actuators are used
- the advantages and disadvantages of actuators.

Fact check

Output and process control: Some output devices show us data (e.g. printers and monitors), but another type of computer device controls a process or a machine. In a control system the computer uses feedback to control a process.

Actuator: An actuator is responsible for moving objects around or controlling a mechanism. In a control system the actuator is controlled by the computer.

Automation: This is a type of control system. The computer controls an actuator, based on feedback from sensors. Automated processes can take place without a human user.

Servomechanism: This is a control system that uses feedback to regulate motion. Instructions tell the computer where an object is supposed to be. The computer measures where the object actually is. The actuator moves the object to bring it to the right place.

Robotics: A robot is a machine controlled by a computer that can move around on its own. The computer, the sensors and the actuator are held in the same case. The robot controls its own motion with the servomechanism method. A robot is designed to do useful tasks.

Computers can control machines that make objects. Using computers in this way has these advantages:

- Computers can control machines very accurately.
- Computers can repeat the same action as many times as you want. They don't get tired.
- Fewer people are needed, which saves money on wages.

These are the disadvantages:

- The equipment can be expensive.
- Computers cannot invent new objects, or work creatively.
- Many people like the variation and uniqueness of hand-made objects.

Check your readiness

This topic includes a number of technical terms. Learn the terms. Write them out with their meanings.

Manufacturing objects

There are two ways in which computers make solid objects: using cutters and using 3D printers. Cutters remove material from a solid block. A 2D cutter cuts flat shapes, or engraves on a surface. 3D printers build up material in layers.

You need to know:
- what 2D and 3D cutters are
- what 3D printers are
- how these devices are used in real life.

Fact check

Cutters: These start with a solid block of material, and cut some away to leave the required shape. They use various methods for this. One example involves a laser beam controlled by a computer. A cutter can cut metal, plastic, silicon, fabric or even diamond. A 2D cutter cuts flat shapes or engraves on a surface. A 3D cutter cuts solid 3D shapes.

Cutting technology: A laser beam is directed at a block of material from one side. The laser melts, burns or vaporises the material. The laser cuts very precisely. It can cut holes, engrave patterns, or melt the material away. In a 2D cutter the laser cuts from one direction only. A 3D cutter uses the same technology as a 2D cutter but the lasers cut from all directions. A 3D cutter can make any shape of object by cutting the material away.

3D printers: These start with nothing and build up layers of material until the required shape has been formed. They make a 3D shape by melting and sticking tiny dots of material together. The dots stick together to make a layer and multiple layers build up to make the object.

3D printers need not be expensive to buy or to use. The cost depends on the type of material used to form the shape.

Check your readiness

Explain how the different technologies described are used to create solid objects.

Output in real life

Modern developments in output technology have had a big impact on our lives. Two main examples are the development of mobile technology and the use of computers to design and create objects.

Fact check

Mobile devices: These are very widespread. Output technology has made mobile devices possible. Some examples are touch screens that are very light in weight and can be used as input and output devices, speakers and headphones, and small actuators that make the phones vibrate.

Printers: Printing has many advantages over on-screen viewing. It gives us a permanent record of output that we can take away from the computer. People like reading from paper instead of a screen and making notes or corrections on paper instead of on a screen.

CAD/CAM: This is used to design objects on the computer screen. Special design software lets you create a 3D image. You can rotate the image on screen to see the shape from all sides. When the design is ready, you send it to a 3D printer that makes the shape. There are advantages to designing objects using the computer instead of making them in real life. Using this system you can:

- make designs cheaply and quickly
- test different designs on the computer before choosing one
- see how well the different parts of an object fit together
- work out what materials are needed and what the cost will be.

When you have created the perfect design you can use the 3D printer, or other cutting technology, to make it.

Key term

CAD/CAM: stands for "computer aided design/computer aided manufacture".

Check your readiness

List the types of output technologies used with mobile devices. Describe the CAD/CAM process and its advantages over other forms of automated manufacture.

4.2 Knowledge test

1. What are the two types of screens in common use nowadays? Describe the differences between these two technologies.

2. What are the advantages and disadvantages of hard copy and soft copy as forms of output? Fill in this table to summarise your answer.

	Hard copy	Soft copy
Advantages		
Disadvantages		

3. What are the two most common types of printer? When would you choose each type of printer?

4. What physical process is used to generate sound output inside a speaker?

5. Explain how an actuator is used as part of a control process.

6. Describe three different types of device that are controlled by the computer and can be used to create solid objects.

7. List the types of output technologies used with mobile devices.

8. What is CAD/CAM and why is it used in industrial design?

4.3 Memory and storage

Primary storage

Primary storage is the active storage in use during the fetch-execute cycle. It is the fastest type of storage for the CPU to use.

Fact check

There are three main types of primary storage:

- **Registers:** These are small active memory areas that can hold one item of data at a time. The content of the registers changes with each fetch-execute cycle.
- **Main memory (RAM):** The content of RAM is stored using electronic charges. RAM is volatile memory. If the computer is turned off, the data stored in RAM is lost.
- **ROM:** This is fixed memory. The content of ROM is set in the factory and cannot be altered. ROM does not use electricity. It is non-volatile.

Primary storage	Advantages	Disadvantages	Uses
Registers	The CPU can access and process the data in the registers with very high speed.	A register can hold only one item at a time. The CPU has very few registers.	A register holds one active instruction and the data that goes with it.
RAM	RAM offers much bigger storage than the registers and much faster access than other forms of storage.	RAM is volatile. It loses all its content when the computer is switched off.	RAM holds the applications and data in current active use.
ROM	ROM is non-volatile.	ROM is read only.	ROM holds start-up instructions.

A computer with a lot of RAM is a fast computer. This is because many instructions can be stored in the fast access area. The computer can easily work through all the instructions in the software without any delay.

Check your readiness

Without referring to your notes or this page, write the table of primary storage types and their advantages and disadvantages.

Measuring storage

Computer memory is organised into bits and bytes. Bytes are the primary units we use to measure the capacity of a storage area.

Fact check

Secondary storage: This is storage outside main memory. Secondary storage does not use active electricity so it is non-volatile. Access to secondary storage is much slower than access to primary storage. Types of secondary storage include hard disk drive, flash memory stick, CD and DVD.

Groups of bytes: How are bytes grouped into kilobytes, megabytes and gigabytes?

- A kilobyte is 1024 bytes
- A megabyte is 1024 kilobytes
- A gigabyte is 1024 megabytes.

Files: Data in secondary storage is organised into files. A file is a collection of data or instructions that all belong together (e.g. a document, an image or a software application). Files are contained in folders. Files may be shown on your screen as small pictures called icons. File size is measured in bytes, kilobytes, megabytes, etc.

Storage capacity: This measures how much data can be stored in secondary storage. Storage capacity is measured in kilobytes, megabytes and gigabytes. Some of the storage capacity will be used up. Some storage will be empty (available). If a file size is smaller than the free storage capacity then you can store the file in that storage area. You should never fill storage to full capacity.

Check your readiness
What units larger than a byte are used to measure storage? What is the exact definition of each unit?

File sizes

From key facts about images, sound files or text files, you can estimate the size of the file in bytes.

Fact check

File size: This is related to data quality. High-quality images and sounds make large files.

Size of a text file: A text file is a series of characters. ASCII code uses one byte to store one character. Unicode uses more bytes: up to four bytes per character.

Size of an image file: An image is made of dots called pixels. The number of bytes depends on how many pixels there are in the image and how many bits are needed for each pixel. High-quality images use more bytes.

Size of a sound or video files: The number of bits needed to store one second of sound or video is called "bit rate". High-quality sound and video has a higher bit rate.

To estimate file sizes:

- Text file – count the number of characters (including spaces). That is the number of bytes.
- Image file – find the height and width of the image in pixels. Multiply height by width to give the total number of pixels. Multiply by the number of bits per pixel to give the total bits.
- Sound or video file – multiply the bit rate per second by the number of seconds of recording.

Bits and bytes: Be careful about the units in use. If you calculate file size in bits divide by 8 to give the number of bytes.

Other factors: Almost all files include additional information as well as the data content. This extra information uses extra storage space. When you estimate file size, remember the real file will be bigger because of this extra information.

Check your readiness

Note the formula you would use to calculate the file size of text, image and sound or video files.

Magnetic storage

Secondary storage is storage outside the CPU and is used to supplement primary storage. Secondary storage gives read/write access and it is non-volatile. Many types of storage use magnetism to record the bits and bytes of data.

You need to know:

- how magnetic storage works
- the different magnetic storage devices and media
- the advantages and disadvantages of magnetic storage.

Fact check

Magnetism: Some materials such as iron oxide are easy to magnetise by bringing a magnet near them. The magnetised spot of material is itself a magnet, with a North pole and a South pole. The direction the magnetised spot faces (NS or SN) can be used to represent one bit of binary data: one direction means 1 and the other means 0.

Magnetic storage: A magnetic storage device converts data into magnetism. The spot stays magnetised after the electric current is taken away. The magnetic dots can be changed, so data can be altered or deleted.

Hard disk drive (HDD): The HDD is a stack of rigid discs held inside the computer casing. The HDD stores data when the computer is switched off.

Portable hard disk: A portable (or removable) hard disk works in the same way as a normal HDD. The only difference is that it is not fixed inside the case – it plugs in externally.

Magnetic tape: This is a long reel of plastic tape. It can be magnetised to store data. To get to the data you want you must wind through the whole tape. Tape is used to make backups.

Key terms

Secondary storage: storage outside the CPU

Non-volatile data: data that is not lost when the computer is switched off.

	Advantages	Disadvantages
Magnetic disk	As it is wired directly to the processor, access to the HDD is quite fast.	An internal hard drive is fixed inside a single computer, so you cannot easily take it away to use on another computer.
Portable hard disk	This can be moved between computers.	Buying a portable hard disk is an additional expense on top of buying a computer.
Magnetic tape	This is inexpensive and it can store a lot of data.	Tape gives very slow access to data.

Check your readiness

Without looking at your notes or this page, write a description of how magnetic storage works. Draw a table of the advantages and disadvantages of the different types of storage.

Optical storage

Optical media provide a convenient alternative to magnetic storage. Although CDs are often read-only, writeable and re-writeable versions are available.

You need to know:
- the way optical secondary storage works
- the different storage devices and media that use optical storage
- the advantages and disadvantages of optical storage.

Fact check

Types of optical storage: There are several types – compact disk (CD), digital versatile disk (DVD) and Blu-Ray.

How optical storage works: Optical storage is read by a light beam. A disk is covered by a thin reflective layer. There are microscopic pits in a spiral pattern on the surface. The disk drive focuses a laser onto the surface. When the laser hits a pit or mark, its reflection is less bright. The difference in light represents the 1s and 0s of digital data.

Dual-layer: Some disks have two spiral tracks, one inside the other.

Storage capacity: The laser that reads the pits can focus on a very small spot. The pits are very small and close together. Although all optical media use small pits, DVDs use smaller pits than CDs and Blu-Ray uses the smallest of all.

"Read only" (CD-ROM or DVD-ROM): An ordinary optical disk is "read only". The pattern of pits is stamped onto the disk when it is made.

"Write once" (CD-R or DVD-R): When you buy the disk it is blank. The CD writer has a strong laser that can burn new data onto the surface of the disk.

Rewriteable (CD-RW or DVD-RW): The disk has a special surface that can be melted. A CD writer has a laser that can melt the surface. This erases the pits so the disk can be re-used.

DVD RAM: A rewriteable disk can be used as RAM. The disc is formatted using concentric circles and is organised into sectors.

Key terms

Read only storage: Stored data can be read by your computer but not changed.

Write-once storage: New data can be stored. But once the data has been 'written' to storage it can't be changed or deleted.

These are the advantages of optical storage:

- Optical media are inexpensive.
- Discs are portable, light and compact.

These are the disadvantages:

- Many CDs are "read only".
- Discs are quite easily broken or scratched.

Check your readiness

Note how optical media store data, and the different forms of access.

Solid state (flash) storage

Solid state or flash memory is extremely compact and useful storage system. The development of modern mobile technology is dependent on flash memory.

Fact check

Solid state storage: Flash memory works by trapping electrons. A "flash" of electricity forces electrons through an insulator. When the electricity stops, the electrons are stuck there. The memory device can detect the stuck electrons. A location with electrons represents a 0. A location without extra electrons represents a 1. This type of storage is called solid state or flash memory.

Write and rewrite: A flash of electricity will put electrons in place. They stay in place when the storage is unplugged. A flash of electricity in the reverse direction will free the trapped electrons. This means flash memory is readable, writeable and deletable.

Use of solid state (flash) storage:

- A USB flash drive is flash memory with a USB plug.
- A solid state drive (SSD) is a large piece of solid state storage fixed inside the computer. It is used in place of a magnetic hard disk drive (HDD).
- Many mobile devices such as smartphones and tablets use solid state (flash) storage.

Solid state (flash) memory has these advantages:

- It is small, light, and strong.
- It stores a lot of data.
- It is erasable and rewriteable.

These are its disadvantages:

- It is more expensive than magnetic memory.
- Some people are concerned about the long-term reliability of flash memory. Nobody can be certain whether it will retain data in the long term.

Check your readiness

Note how flash memory works and list its advantages. What modern technologies use flash memory?

Use and choice of storage

The right storage choice depends on context. Magnetic tape is used for backup. Cloud storage allows you to access storage remotely from any device with an Internet connection.

You need to know:
- how different types of storage are used in real life
- the right storage choices for different real-life needs.

Fact check

Choosing storage: When choosing storage, you should think about:

- Capacity – how much data do you need to store?
- Portability – do you need to move your data between computers?
- Cost – how do the options compare?
- Speed of access – hard drives wired into the computer are the fastest, tape is the slowest.
- Reliability and durability – is there a risk of loss or damage?

Backups: A backup is a second copy of your data you set aside. If your main data is lost, you can use the backup to restore your lost data. Storage media for backup should be reliable and inexpensive with high capacity. Magnetic tape is a good choice.

Cloud storage: The data is sent along an Internet connection to be stored. The data is stored by an Internet company on its own computers.

These are the advantages of cloud storage:

- You can access your data from any device with an Internet connection.
- The Internet company backs up the data so it is not at risk of being lost.
- Cloud storage doesn't take up any space on your own device, so it is very popular for use with smartphones and tablets   .

There are also disadvantages:

- There are some concerns about privacy because your data is held by someone else.
- You cannot access the data if your Internet connection fails.

Check your readiness

This page lists five factors you should think about when choosing storage. Review all the storage options you have learned against these five factors.

4.3 Knowledge test

1. What is volatile memory?

2. Why does a computer processor need both ROM and RAM?

3. What is the difference between primary and secondary storage?

4. How many bytes are in a megabyte? You may use a calculator.

5. A text file has 10 pages, with 2000 characters on each page. Estimate the size of the file in bytes.

6. To estimate the size of a bitmap file, what two facts would you need to know about how the image is stored?

7. The size of a sound file is calculated using the bit rate. What does "bit rate" mean?

8. Describe how magnetic storage retains data even when it is not connected to an electrical power source.

9. CDs, DVDs and Blu-ray disks all use optical methods of storage. What is the difference between these three?

10. Flash memory is more popular than magnetic and optical storage nowadays. What features of flash memory make it such a good choice? What features limit its use?

11. Why is magnetic tape suitable for backup – but not many other uses?

12. What is cloud storage?

Exam preparation

1. Use the information contained in topics 4.1, 4.2 and 4.3 to describe the following actions in relation to a computer system:
   a Input
   b Output
   c Storage

Exam-style questions

1. a Name two manual input devices and give **two** advantages and **two** disadvantages of each.
   b Name, compare and contrast **two** methods of automatic data input.
   c i One type of touch screen technology is infra-red. State one advantage and one disadvantage of this type of touch screen.
     ii Name another type of touch screen technology and explain how it differs from the infra-red type.
2. a For each of the following printer types, give two benefits, two drawbacks and state where you would expect to find each one.
     i Inkjet
     ii Laser.
   b Objects can be designed on a computer screen using CAD software.
     i State two benefits of designing objects in this way.
     ii Name two hardware devices that could be connected to the system to produce the solid output.
3. a Compare RAM and ROM, giving **two** features and **one** purpose of each.
   b For the following types of storage, give an example, **one** advantage, **one** disadvantage and **one** possible use of each.
     i Magnetic
     ii Optical
     iii Solid state.

5 Software

This page summarises what you will learn about software. Tick the boxes on this page when you are confident you have learned each item.

5.1 Systems software

TICK WHEN YOU HAVE LEARNED:

- [ ] what software is
- [ ] the difference between applications software and systems software
- [ ] what an operating system is
- [ ] the functions of an operating system
- [ ] what an interrupt is and why interrupts must be handled by the computer system.

5.2 Computer languages

TICK WHEN YOU HAVE LEARNED:

- [ ] what programming languages are
- [ ] the difference between machine code and program code
- [ ] what low-level languages are
- [ ] the meaning of assembly language
- [ ] what compilers and interpreters are
- [ ] the advantages of compiled and interpreted languages.

5.1 Systems software

What is software?

Software is the general name for the instructions that tell the computer what to do. Systems software is software that controls the computer system itself.

You need to know:
- what software is
- the difference between applications software and systems software.

Fact check

Software: A software file is a collection of instruction codes. To use software on your computer, you must load it and run it.

Load software: All the instruction codes in the software file are copied from secondary storage into main memory (RAM).

Run software: The CPU fetches the instructions one at a time and executes them.

Types of software: There are two types. Application software carries out tasks for the user. Modern applications are often called apps. Systems software maintains the functioning of the computer.

Systems software: This makes the computer work properly. The instruction codes in systems software help the CPU to run the computer system, for example to:

- start up the computer
- load and run applications chosen by the user
- control the flow of data from the input devices and to the output devices
- organise memory and storage.

Typically you do not have to load and run systems software. It is loaded into RAM when you start up the computer. It runs automatically all the time the computer is working.

How software is made: Software is created by programmers. A programmer writes a program using a programming language. The program is then converted into binary instruction codes that the CPU can understand.

Check your readiness

List the main tasks of systems software.

Operating systems

An operating system is the collection of all the systems software needed to run the computer. It is loaded into RAM when the computer is powered up, and remains there while it is in use.

You need to know:
- what an operating system is and what it does
- that there are different operating systems.

Fact check

Operating system: Every computer needs systems software. In modern computers, all the systems software is collected into one large file. This is called the operating system. The operating system runs in RAM all the time the computer is switched on. It makes the computer work properly.

Boot up: When you switch the computer on, the CPU loads the operating system into RAM. It gets the start-up instructions from ROM. The start-up instructions tell the computer to connect to storage. The computer loads the rest of the operating system from storage. This is called booting up or starting up.

ROM BIOS: On a PC, the start-up instructions in ROM are called the BIOS. BIOS stands for "basic input/output system". The BIOS instructions are loaded and executed as soon as the computer starts up. These instructions let the processor control the computer's peripherals. Then the processor can get the rest of the operating system from secondary storage.

Different operating systems: There are many different operating systems. Microsoft Windows is the most widely used operating system in the world. Most laptop and desktop computers use Windows. Android is an operating system used on many mobile devices such as tablets and smartphones.

Compatible software: Software written for one operating system cannot run on a computer that uses a different operating system. The software is not compatible with the operating system. You have to check operating system compatibility when you buy or download software.

Check your readiness

Describe what happens during the boot-up process and the reason it is important to know about the different operating systems that are available.

Functions of an operating system

Operating systems have many functions which are all required in order for a modern computer to work properly. The interface allows you to control what the computer does.

You need to know:
- the functions of an operating system
- what an interrupt is and why interrupts must be handled by the computer system.

Fact check

Functions: The job of an operating system is to make the computer work properly. Its tasks include:
- controlling hardware
- providing a user interface
- loading and running software
- handling errors and problems.

Controlling hardware: The operating system lets the CPU communicate with the peripherals such as the keyboard or monitor. The computer gets data from peripherals and sends control signals to the peripherals.

User interface: The user interface is what you experience when you use the computer – for example looking at the screen display and using the keyboard. The interface puts the output of the computer into a form you can understand. It also turns your actions into commands that control the computer.

Loading and running applications: Most computers nowadays have a graphical user interface (GUI). You might use a mouse pointer or you might use a touch screen. A GUI has icons that stand for applications. Using the interface, you can select an icon. The operating system will load and run that application.

Handling errors: The operating system responds to errors such as hardware failure or mistakes by the user. When the operating system finds an error it will typically identify the error and interrupt your work with an error message.

Interrupts: An interrupt is a signal that stops the current program. It points the processor to a new instruction in memory. Errors can cause interrupts. Communications from peripherals or from other computers can interrupt the processes on your computer.

Check your readiness

List and describe the main tasks of an operating system.

5.1 Knowledge test

1. What are the two types of software, and what is the difference between them?

2. What is the difference between loading and running software?

3. When you buy software you need to know what operating system it is compatible with. Explain why.

4. State four functions of an operating system.

5. What happens during boot up?

6. What are interrupts?

5.2 Computer languages

Programming languages

The instructions inside the computer are held as machine code. It is difficult for the human user to read and write machine code. Programming languages were invented to make it easier for us to write instructions for the computer.

Fact check

The fetch-execute cycle: During the fetch-execute cycle the processor fetches instructions one at a time from main memory. These instructions are stored using code numbers. The processor executes (carries out) the instructions.

Machine code: Instructions are stored in the main memory as binary numbers. The number code that matches binary numbers to instructions is called "machine code". A computer file made of machine code is called an executable file. Software applications are stored as executable files. When you run the executable file the instructions are carried out.

Writing new instructions: To make new software you have to write the instructions. You could just write the machine code using binary or hexadecimal numbers that stand for instruction codes, data and memory addresses.

Programming languages: It is difficult to write a program just using numbers. Programming languages were invented to make it easier to write software. Computer languages let you write software instructions using words and symbols instead of binary code. These instructions are called program code.

Translation: After you have written the program code it must be converted to machine code. Then you can run the code. The computer understands machine code. It can carry out the instructions. The process of turning a program into machine code is called translation.

Check your readiness

Explain the different uses of machine code and program code, and why both are needed when a person writes a program in a computer language.

Low-level languages

Low-level languages are similar to machine code, but are easier than machine code for human beings to understand. They are not the most commonly used computer languages but they do have advantages. Assembly language is the most common low-level language.

Fact check

What is a low-level language? A language that is similar to machine code is called a low-level language. Assembly language is a low-level language.

Assembly language: Assembly language uses short text words (usually three letters). Each word matches an instruction in machine code. For example, the instruction to add a number to a stored value in assembly language might be the word "ADD". Assembly language instructions may also include hexadecimal numbers. These stand for the data (e.g. the number to add).

Translation: A piece of software called an assembler is used to translate assembly language into machine code. The words of assembly language match up exactly to the binary numbers of machine code. This means translation is very quick and easy.

Low-level languages have some disadvantages:

- It is quite difficult to write a program in a low-level language compared to other programming languages.
- Many low-level languages will only work with one make of computer.

Programmers still use low-level languages for some tasks because these languages have advantages:

- Low-level languages match the instruction set closely.
- Their close match to the instruction set can give the programmer better control over the processor.
- Programs written in low-level languages are typically quick to run on the processor.

Use of low-level languages: Assembly language is often used to create device drivers for new types of hardware. Device drivers are instructions that let the CPU communicate with peripherals.

Check your readiness

Without looking at your notes or this page, list the main features and uses of assembly language and its advantages over machine code and other programming languages.

High-level languages

High-level languages are easier to write than assembly language. Different languages are either compiled or interpreted.

You need to know:
- what compilers and interpreters are
- the advantages of compiled and interpreted languages.

Fact check

High-level languages: A high-level language is an alternative to low-level assembly language. Unlike a low-level language, a high-level language is not very similar to machine code. High-level languages are easier for people to understand and they are not tied to a particular instruction set.

Different languages are designed for different purposes. Users choose what language to use by considering what their task is. Python is a straight forward language that is suitable for use when learning programming.

Translating into machine code: High-level languages can be translated in two ways: with a compiler or with an interpreter.

Compiler: Languages translated by a compiler are called compiled languages. A compiler turns the whole program into machine code. The machine code is saved to storage as an executable file. To carry out the instructions you must load and run the executable file, as with any other application.

These are the advantages of using compilers:

- You end up with an executable file.
- You can sell or share the file.
- Anyone can run it.

Using a compiler also has disadvantages:

- You must compile the program to make a new executable file every time you make a change.
- There is a risk of confusion between versions.

Interpreter: Languages translated by interpreters are called interpreted languages. An interpreter translates the code one action at a time. When the action is done, the interpreter moves on to the next part of the program code. The interpreter does not save any machine code. It does not make an executable file.

The advantage of an interpreter is that if you make a change to your code, you can run the program and see the effect right away. These are the disadvantages of interpreters:

- The program will not run unless you have the interpreter on your computer.
- There is no executable file to sell or share.

Check your readiness

List the differences between compiled and interpreted languages. Draw a table of advantages and disadvantages of compilers and interpreters.

5.2 Knowledge test

1. What is machine code? Why is it rare to write programs in machine code?

2. What is the difference between assembly language and machine code?

3. What are the advantages and disadvantages of assembly language compared to high-level language code?

4. Why must program code be translated before it can be executed?

5. What is the difference between a compiled and interpreted language?

6. Why is it useful for a programmer to know a range of different computer languages?

7. What are the advantages and disadvantages of compiled languages?

8. What are the advantages and disadvantages of interpreted languages?

Exam preparation

1. Use the information contained in topic 5.1 to describe the following:
   a Applications software
   b Systems software.

Exam-style questions

1. The operating system is an example of system software.
   a Name **four** operations carried out by an operating system.
   b For any **two** of the operations listed for part **a**:
      i   describe its purpose
      ii   give **one** example.
   c State the purpose of an interrupt.
2. a Compare high-level languages with low-level languages from the point of view of a programmer.
   b Name the two types of software used to translate your program into a form the computer can understand.
   c For one of the types of software named in part **b**:
      i   describe its method of operation
      ii state one benefit of this type of translation
      iii state one problem with this type of translation.

6 Security

This page summarises what you will learn about security. Tick the boxes on this page when you are confident you have learned each item.

6.1 Security threats

TICK WHEN YOU HAVE LEARNED:

- [ ] what data security is
- [ ] why it is important to protect systems against online attacks
- [ ] what privacy and integrity of data are
- [ ] internal threats and how to protect against them
- [ ] external threats and how to protect against them
- [ ] the different types of crime and malpractice
- [ ] the meaning of the technical terms "phishing", "pharming" and "denial of service".

6.2 Security protection

TICK WHEN YOU HAVE LEARNED:

- [ ] ways to prove identity
- [ ] what a firewall is
- [ ] what a proxy server is
- [ ] what a security protocol is
- [ ] how certification is used in the handshake process
- [ ] what encryption is
- [ ] the difference between symmetric and asymmetric encryption
- [ ] how security methods are used in real life.

6.1 Security threats

Data security

Data security involves protecting the integrity and privacy of data. Data integrity means keeping the data complete and undamaged. Privacy means preventing unauthorised access to the data.

You need to know:
- what data security is
- the main threats to data security.

Fact check

Data is valuable: Collecting and processing data takes time and money. Good data is helpful and useful. People and businesses want to protect the privacy and integrity of their data.

Privacy: Protecting data privacy means protecting data from unauthorised access.

Integrity: Protecting data integrity means protecting data from being lost, damaged or corrupted.

Loss: Data loss means you don't have the data any more. It can be caused by loss of the storage media, damage to storage, accidental deletion or faults in the hardware or software you use.

Corruption: Data corruption means the data has been damaged or changed. If data is corrupted, it may no longer be accurate. If it is badly corrupted, the computer can no longer read the data. Corruption can be caused by faults in transmission or damage to the storage medium.

Unauthorised access: Some people have permission to see or alter data. Other people do not have permission. If people access data without permission this is called unauthorised access. They might look at it, copy it or make changes to it.

Key terms
Data security: refers to protecting the privacy and integrity of data on computer systems

Privacy: when data is only seen by people with permission. Data is not disclosed outside of this limit.

Integrity: means that data is kept complete and undamaged so it can be accessed in full when you need it.

> ### Check your readiness
> List the main reasons for data security. Explain the difference between loss, corruption and unauthorised access.

Security threats

Companies are affected by internal and external threats to security. Internal threats include hardware and software failure and malpractice. External threats include accidents and attacks.

You need to know:
- the internal issues that can harm data security
- the external that can harm data security.

Fact check

Internal threats: These are problems within a company. Good business practice can reduce internal threats. Here are some examples:

- Hardware faults can include faults in storage devices, storage media, data transmission media and fire damage. Hardware faults can be reduced by buying good quality equipment, having fire protection measures and training people to use equipment safely.

- Software faults can lead to loss of data. Software faults can be prevented by buying good-quality software and training people to use the software properly.
- Malpractice usually involves the human users of a computer system making mistakes. For example they might break equipment, use the software in the wrong way or damage storage media. Good training and support can reduce malpractice.
- Crime means a deliberate intention to cause harm, for example through vandalism or theft. Crime by employees can be reduced by effective recruitment and management of staff.

External threats can also cause problems:

- Events outside a company's control (e.g. floods, earthquakes or power cuts) can have a negative effect on computer systems. Good business practice can protect against damage from many of these. Protective building design can help. Some companies have their own electricity generators to ensure no loss of power. All data should be backed up.
- External attacks are threats caused by deliberate human action. These include crime and fraud, malware and hackers. Company security systems aim to protect systems from external attacks.

Check your readiness

List the main internal and external threats and how companies can plan to keep the effects of these threats to a minimum.

Malpractice and crime

Malpractice (not doing work properly due to careless behaviour) and crime (deliberate action) can result in threats to data, including threats due to unauthorised access and data being deleted or changed without permission.

You need to know:
- the data security threats that are a result of malpractice and crime.

Fact check

Unauthorised access: If someone has unauthorised access to data it means that the person can see or alter data without permission. It could be someone inside the company. It could be someone outside the company using a computer communication link.

Viewing or copying: When people gain access to a computer system they might simply look at data. They might make a copy of the data. It can be hard to spot this type of access because the data has not changed.

Deleting or changing: When people gain access to a computer system they might delete the data or make changes to it. For example, someone might change the data on a bank computer to increase the amount in his or her own bank account.

Malpractice: Malpractice means not doing your work properly. Malpractice can be a threat to data security. Some examples of malpractice are:

- leaving the computer logged on when you go out of the room, so that someone else can access your files
- telling someone else your password, so that the computer system is no longer secure
- downloading software from the Internet or opening a damaging email, which can put malware onto the computer.

Crime: This is more serious than malpractice. Crime involves deliberate actions to cause harm. Some examples are:

- piracy – taking a copy of music, games, movies etc., without permission
- hacking – gaining unauthorised access to ICT systems
- creating and distributing malware
- identity theft – stealing someone else's personal details and pretending to be that person.

Check your readiness

List examples of malpractice and crime. Explain how each can lead to loss of data privacy or integrity.

Online attacks

There are some specialist terms that refer to particular online attacks: "phishing", "pharming", "denial of service (DoS)" and the more serious "distributed denial of service (DDoS)".

You need to know:
- why it is important to protect systems against online attacks
- the meaning of technical terms "phishing", "pharming" and "denial of service (DoS)" or "distributed denial of service (DDos)".

Fact check

DoS: A DoS attack is a way of harming a company's computer services. It works by flooding the computer with many requests or messages. A DoS attack might make the computer go very slowly.

DDoS: A more serious attack is called a DDoS. The messages seem to be being sent from hundreds of different addresses and this makes it harder to block them all.

Identity theft: When a criminal finds out your personal details, the criminal can then use this information to pretend to be you online. The person can spend your money to buy things and send messages, pretending to be you.

Phishing: This describes sending a fake email or other message. It will look like an email from a real company (e.g. your bank). It might ask for your password or other details. Criminals have sent the email to try to get your details so they can commit identity theft.

Pharming: This is typically done by making a fake website. It will look like the website of a real company (e.g. one that sells products online). If you log on, then enter information, such as your name and bank details, criminals find out that information. Opening a malware file or clicking on a link in an email can lead you to one of these fake websites.

Check your readiness

List the technical terms relating to online attacks that you have learned. Give a definition of each term. How do criminals hope to gain from each of the activities described?

6.1 Knowledge test

1. What is data integrity?

2. What is data privacy?

3. Explain the difference between data loss, data corruption and unauthorised access to data.

4. Describe the main internal threats to data security. How can companies limit their impact?

5. Describe the main external threats to data security. How can companies limit their impact?

6. List examples of malpractice and how they can harm data security.

7. What is pharming and why do people do it?

8. What is phishing and why do people do it?

9. Explain what a DDoS attack is.

6.2 Security protection

Proof of identity

When you use a computer system you often have to provide your identity (ID). ID checks include passwords, ID cards and biometrics.

You need to know:
- what proof of identity is
- ways to prove identity.

Fact check

Ways to prove identity: Proof of identity is important for data security, to control access to data and to prevent identity theft. Proving or checking identity is also known as authentication. The main methods used for proof of identity are:

- passwords
- biometrics
- ID cards.

Passwords: A password is a series of characters or numbers you have chosen. When you have to prove who you are, you enter the password.

Strong passwords: Criminals will try to gain access to a system by guessing passwords. For this reason, you should use a password that is hard to guess. This is called a strong password. The strongest passwords use a mix of letters, numbers and other characters.

The advantages of passwords are that they don't cost anything and are easy to use. The disadvantages are that people sometimes forget their password; and that some people's passwords are easy for other people to guess.

ID card: An alternative to a password is an ID card. It can be read by a special card reader. An ID card can be checked by a person, as well as read by a computer. The card often has your photograph on it for use as an additional check.

The advantage of using an ID card is that is can be read by a person or computerised system. The disadvantage is that it can easily be lost.

Biometric check: Biometric means a physical characteristic. A biometric check means proving your identity by means of physical features. That could include finger print, thumb print or palm print, and an iris scan (checking the pattern of colours in your eye).

The advantage of biometric checks is that it is difficult or impossible for someone else to steal your biometric features. The disadvantage is that this method needs expensive equipment.

Many companies use more than one proof of identify to create a more secure system.

Check your readiness

Describe the meaning of each type of identity check. Explain the advantages and disadvantages of each one.

Firewalls

The Internet is a source of security risks and unsuitable content. A proxy server simplifies Internet communication by making a local copy of websites. A firewall checks all Internet content as it passes to or from a local area network (LAN).

Fact check

The Internet is a source of malware and other risks. This damaging content might get onto a LAN through an Internet connection. Proxy servers and firewalls are ways to prevent this from happening.

Proxy server: Many organisations offer access to the Internet through a router. A user will request data from a website. The proxy server will go to the website once and get the data the user wants. The data will be stored on the proxy server. When the user looks at the website, they look at the copy on the proxy server. They will look at the copy every time they go to that website. If the website changes, then the proxy server will update the copy. This means that users in that company do not make a connection directly to the web pages they look at. They connect to a nearby computer instead of a distant website. This has some advantages:

- The connection is faster.
- Users are protected.
- Their use of the Internet can be checked.

Firewall: A firewall is a barrier between the Internet and the local network. The firewall checks all the data that passes in or out of the local network. It will only transmit data if it passes all the checks. The advantage of this is that computers in the local network are protected from malware.

All data goes through the firewall device to get in or out of the network. A firewall typically includes hardware and software. It contains a processor. The firewall software tells the processor how to check the data that passes through the device.

Key term
Router: the device that joins a LAN to the Internet.

> **Check your readiness**
> Explain the function and advantages of a firewall and a proxy server.

Security protocols

Security protocols are standard methods for keeping long-distance communications secure. The most common is transport layer security (TLS). It includes standards for encryption and authentication.

Fact check

Protocols: A protocol is a standard method of communication. Computers that use the same protocols can communicate with each other. Security protocols make sure communications are safe and secure.

Transport layer security (TLS): Transport layer protocols control the start and end of a communication link.

Secure sockets layer (SSL): This is a protocol that was used before TLS. It has the same general purpose. It is not as up to date and is less secure. The two are grouped together as TLS/SSL. Not all Internet communication is protected by TLS/SSL.

TLS makes communication private. If you send a message to a computer only that computer can read it, even if it passes through lots of connections to get there.

TLS protocol has two parts:

- TLS record protocol breaks the communication down into parts called records.
- TLS handshake protocol controls how computers recognise each other.

Handshake: A handshake protocol is a signal sent between two devices at the start of communication. It includes authentication and encryption.

Authentication: A genuine website has a security certificate, issued by a certificate authority (CA). A security certificate is a bit like an electronic ID card that proves the computer's identity. During handshake each computer checks the security certificate of the other computer.

Certification authority (CA): A CA is an organisation that everyone trusts. It issues certificates to websites. The CA will check a company is genuine before it gives a certificate.

Check your readiness

Explain how a handshake ensures authentication and describe the role of the CA.

Encryption

Some messages are encrypted before being sent over the Internet. Encryption uses a key. If the encryption and decryption keys are the same that is symmetric encryption. If they are different that is asymmetric encryption.

You need to know:
- what encryption is
- the difference between symmetric and asymmetric encryption.

Fact check

Why encryption takes place: An Internet message goes through lots of connections and devices on its way to its destination. If it was in plain text it could be read by anyone. Instead it is encrypted.

How encryption takes place: Encryption is done by your computer before the message is sent. You don't see the scrambled text. You don't have to understand the code.

Two computers are involved in encryption. The sender encrypts the message (and then sends it). The receiver decrypts the message (when it receives it).

Encryption key: Encryption uses a secret code called a key. The key tells the computer how to encrypt and decrypt your message. Only a computer that has the right key can read the message.

Key terms

Plain text: ordinary words and numbers

Cypher text: text that has been scrambled or disguised using a secret code

Symmetric encryption: In symmetric encryption, one key is used for both encryption and decryption. The sender and receiver share the same key. However, to share the key they must send it down an Internet connection. Hackers might get hold of the key on the way.

Asymmetric encryption: In asymmetric encryption there are two keys:

- A public key is used for encryption. Anyone can have that key.
- A private key is used for decryption. It is kept safe on one computer.

The private decryption key is never sent out. Asymmetric encryption is safer than symmetric encryption.

Check your readiness

Explain how a key is used in encryption. What is the advantage of asymmetric encryption?

Security examples

The security methods you have learned about make many modern uses of the Internet more safe and reliable. Banking, e-commerce, teleworking and cloud services all depend on good security systems.

You need to know:
- how security methods are used in real life.

Fact check

Banking: Online banking lets you do all your banking tasks on the Internet. Every time you tell the bank to make a payment you must prove your identity. It is important to make sure nobody else can make payments with your money. Online banking uses passwords, encryption and security protocols to protect your details.

E-commerce: E-commerce means buying and selling things over the Internet. To buy things over the Internet you must send your bank account details to a website. You must trust the people who run the website to keep your details secure. Handshake protocols and authentication help you to trust the website.

Teleworking: Teleworkers work from home. They connect to their workplace using a long-distance link. They need a safe and secure link from their home computer to their work computer. Data sent between the two computers is encrypted.

These are the advantages of teleworking:

- it saves travel time
- it reduces road congestion and pollution
- people are able to work when the office is closed
- the employer can have smaller offices.

Disadvantages of teleworking include the following:

- it is not suitable for all types of work
- management, leadership and supervision are more difficult
- teleworking makes teamwork more difficult
- there is less social contact for workers.

Cloud services: Cloud storage lets you save your work over an Internet connection. You do not want anyone else to access your work. Cloud services use passwords and encryption.

Check your readiness

Explain how ID checks, passwords, encryption and security protocols help to maintain modern computer services.

6.2 Knowledge test

1. What are the main methods for proving identify?

2. Why might a company use more than one method to provide identity?

3. What is the job of a firewall?

4. How does the use of a proxy server improve the way users access the internet?

5. What is a security protocol?

6. Explain how a handshake ensures authentication.

7. What is encryption?

8. What is the advantage of asymmetric encryption?

9. Describe a useful modern function of computers that relies on good security protocols.

Exam preparation

1. Use the information contained in topic 6.1 to describe the following:
   a Data privacy
   b Data integrity
   c Data security.

Exam-style questions

1. Computer crime is a serious threat to anyone who uses computers. Explain the following terms and state the possible consequences:
   a Pharming
   b Phishing
   c Hacking.
2. a Describe what is meant by authentication in the context of using a computer system.
   b Name **three** methods of authentications and give **one** advantage and **one** disadvantage of each.
3. a State **three** functions of a firewall.
   b State and describe one method that is used to prevent data being read by unauthorised users.

7 Ethics

This page summarises what you will learn about ethics and computers. Tick the boxes on this page when you are confident you have learned each item.

7.1 Ethics

TICK WHEN YOU HAVE LEARNED:

- [ ] key issues in computer ethics
- [ ] what intellectual property is
- [ ] the importance of copyright and plagiarism
- [ ] the problem of plagiarism and how to avoid it
- [ ] the different types of free software, freeware and shareware
- [ ] what hacking is.

Ethics

The use of computers brings new ethical challenges because it makes some actions easier than they used to be. The Internet brings us into contact with people who may have very different beliefs and standards from our own.

You need to know:
- why the use of computers has brought new ethical challenges
- key issues in computer ethics.

Fact check

Ethics – views and issues: Ethics is the study of right and wrong. People disagree about what behaviour is ethical. People's views about ethics are influenced by religion, politics, traditions and family life. The Internet lets us interact with people all over the world. They may have different views from the ones we are used to. This means computers make us think hard about ethical issues.

Ethics is not the same as law. Some unethical actions are against the law, but some unethical actions are lawful. That does not make them right. Technology is always changing. Sometimes the law has not caught up with technology. New laws might be needed, and until that time, legal protection may be unclear. Sometimes computers make it easier for criminals to break laws.

Easy copying: Computers make many tasks much easier than they used to be. An example is copying. Data on the computer is very easy to copy. This is very useful and so we make copies all the time. However, copying brings ethical challenges. Do we always have permission to copy other people's work? What are the rules about copying?

For all of these reasons, the use of computers brings ethical challenges and risks.

> **Check your readiness**
>
> Describe the ethical issues raised by the increased use of computers.

Copyright

If you have intellectual property rights (IPR) it means that nobody is allowed to copy your intellectual property (the products of your own creative work) without your permission. To use the content of someone else's intellectual property (IP) you must have permission and may have to pay for it. In many cases, you can quote a small extract for free if you give credit to the source. If you copy someone's else's work then claim it as your own work, that is plagiarism.

You need to know:
- what intellectual property is
- the significance of copyright and plagiarism.

Fact check

Intellectual property (IP): Your IP is anything you made with your own ideas and creativity. It could be music, a book, an invention or a design. You have IPR. Nobody is allowed to copy your intellectual property without your permission. IPR is protected by international agreements.

Copyright: Copyright law covers text, music, video and software. You can only copy this content if you have permission. Generally, to get permission you have to pay. The people who made the content may have worked hard. If you make a copy without paying, they do not get any reward.

Plagiarism: If you make a copy of someone's work and then pretend it is your own, that is plagiarism. You can be in legal trouble, and you can fail your school course.

Fair use: Despite copyright law you are allowed to make some use of digital material. The laws vary between countries but the general term is "fair use". In general, it is fair to use a copy in your own work if:

- you only take a small part of the work
- you credit the original source.

Referencing the source: If you copy and paste someone else's material (such as text, tables, pictures or graphs) into your school work you must say where the material came from. Your teachers will explain how to give proper references in your work.

Check your readiness

It is easy to make copies of digital content using computer equipment. Explain how these copies are covered by laws on IPR, copyright and plagiarism.

Free software

Software is covered by IPR. However, some software is available for free. Different types of software are offered under different terms.

You need to know:
- the different types of free software, freeware and shareware.

Fact check

"Free": In the context of software, "free" can have different meanings as follows:

- You don't have to pay for the software. However, there may be restrictions, for example you are not allowed to modify it or make copies for others to use.
- You might or might not have to pay for the software. Once you have it, you are free to do anything you like with it, including modify it, or give or sell copies to others.

Open source: A program written in a computer language is called source code. Source code is compiled to make an executable file of machine code. Usually, when you buy software you only get the machine code. With open source software you can get the source code too. You are allowed to make changes to the code. You can make new versions of the software. You can even sell them.

Public domain: Software in the public domain is free for anyone to use. The programmers have given up their IPR. Nobody has any legal ownership of the software. It can be used for anything.

Free software: This is open source software that you can use, copy, adapt or even re-sell. In some cases you have to pay for it, but you might not have to. It may be in the public domain or not.

Freeware: Freeware is software that is free of charge – you don't pay for it. It is not in the public domain. It is not open source software. The owners retain their IPR.

Shareware: Shareware is similar to freeware. It is not in the public domain. It is free of charge. Shareware is different from freeware because you do pay for it in certain circumstances – there are often restrictions on the work you can do with shareware and to remove these restrictions you must pay for the software.

Check your readiness

Describe the differences between freeware, shareware and free software.

Hackers and crackers

Hackers break into computer systems. Some do this without permission and this is breaking the law. Hackers can use virus software to make it easier to break into systems.

You need to know:
- what hacking is
- the ethical issues arising from hacking.

Fact check

Meaning of the word "hacker": The word "hacker" is used in different ways. It might be used to refer to a person who likes to investigate computer systems, to understand them better. More often, it describes a person who breaks into computer systems to steal or change data.

Types of hackers:

- **Black hat** hackers break into computer systems without permission. They are also called crackers. They typically do this to obtain information secretly or to take money.
- **White hat** hackers break into computer systems with permission, to test the security.
- **Grey hat** hackers may break into systems without permission. However, they may not do any damage. They may be testing their own skills.

Some hackers cause a lot of damage to computer systems. In extreme cases this can lead to financial loss or harm to people. If you hack into computer systems without permission you are at risk of prosecution. Combatting hacking can cost businesses a lot of money.

Malware: Malware is software that can damage the computer system. The most common example is a virus. Some programmers make malware for a prank or a joke. Others make malware to help them hack into computer systems. A system with malware on it can be easier to break into. For example "spyware" will record what you type when you are using the computer. This data is then sent to the person who made the spyware. They can analyse it to find out your password and other personal details.

> **Check your readiness**
> Define the three types of hacker. Explain how malware can help hackers to break into computer systems.

7 Knowledge test

1. What is the difference between unethical behaviour and illegal behaviour?

2. Why might the increase in use of computers bring the need for new laws?

3. How do the laws on IPR and copyright protect people who make creative works?

4. What is plagiarism? How have computers made plagiarism easier?

5. Describe the differences between freeware, shareware and free software.

6. What are the three types of hacker defined by "hat colour", and what are the differences between each type?

Exam preparation

1. Use the information contained in chapter 7 to describe the meaning of computer ethics.

Exam-style questions

1. **a** Describe the term "copyright".
   b Explain the benefits of copyright to the copyright holder.
2. Define each of the following types of software:
   a Free software
   b Freeware
   c Shareware.
3. Describe how hacking may be used to improve computer security.

8 Programming

This page summarises what you will learn about programming. Tick the boxes on this page when you are confident you have learned each item.

8.1 Introduction to programming

TICK WHEN YOU HAVE LEARNED:

- [ ] how to start up Python and open the software
- [ ] the main features of Python
- [ ] what an IDE is
- [ ] what an algorithm is
- [ ] how flowcharts are used to show algorithms
- [ ] how pseudocode is used to show algorithms
- [ ] the advantages of different ways of showing algorithms.

8.2 Begin coding

TICK WHEN YOU HAVE LEARNED:

- [ ] how to write and run a Python program
- [ ] how to input a value to a variable
- [ ] how to assign a value to a variable
- [ ] what data types are and how to change data type
- [ ] how to use arithmetic operators in calculations
- [ ] how to output strings and variables
- [ ] how to create pseudocode algorithms with variables
- [ ] how to create flowchart algorithms with variables.

8.3 Selection

TICK WHEN YOU HAVE LEARNED:

- [ ] what a logical test is
- [ ] how to use relational operators to make logical tests
- [ ] how to use decision boxes in flowchart algorithms
- [ ] how to write Python programs using `if... else`
- [ ] how to write Python programs using `elif`
- [ ] how to write pseudocode algorithms using `IF.. ELSE.. ENDIF`
- [ ] how to write pseudocode algorithms using `CASE... ENDCASE`.

8.4 Repetition

TICK WHEN YOU HAVE LEARNED:

- [ ] what a counter-controlled loop is
- [ ] what a condition-controlled loop is
- [ ] how to draw flowcharts with loops
- [ ] how to write Python programs with `for` loops
- [ ] how to write Python programs with `while` loops
- [ ] how to write pseudocode algorithms with `FOR` loops
- [ ] how to write pseudocode algorithms with `WHILE` loops
- [ ] how to write pseudocode algorithms with `REPEAT` loops.

8.5 Data structures

TICK WHEN YOU HAVE LEARNED:

- [ ] what a list is
- [ ] how to make an empty list
- [ ] how to make a list with several elements
- [ ] how to append elements to a list
- [ ] how to print the elements of a list using a for loop
- [ ] what an array is
- [ ] how to declare an array with a given number of elements
- [ ] how to print the elements of an array with a for loop.

8.1 Introduction to programming

Introduction to Python

To practise using programming features you will write programs in a language called Python.

Python

Python is a programming language. It is:
- an interpreted language
- free to use
- open source.

To download Python go to the main Python website https://www.python.org/.

There are several versions of Python. The examples in this book match any version that starts with the number 3.

Integrated development environment (IDE): An IDE is software that lets you prepare your program code and save it as a file. A typical IDE has many useful features. For example:
- the use of colour to show different types of code
- a command to execute (run) the program
- error messages to identify syntax or run-time errors.

The Python IDE is called IDLE. IDLE has two windows.

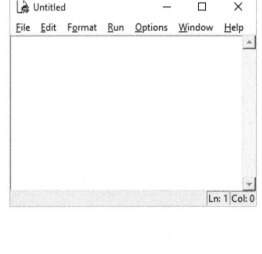

It has a edit window, where you can enter and save a program file.

It also has the "Python Shell" window. This is where any output will appear.

When you start IDLE only one of these windows will appear. Use the menu bars at the top of the windows to open and close the windows. You can also start a new file or open a file you already made.

If both windows are closed Python shuts down.

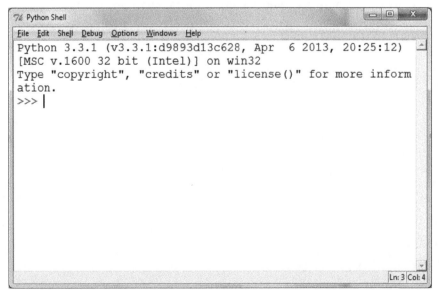

Check your readiness

You should be able to start up Python and recognise the two windows. You should be able to use the menu bars to open and close the windows.

Algorithms

An algorithm sets out the logical steps needed to solve a problem. Programmers prepare algorithms before they start coding. Pseudocode and flowcharts are used to describe algorithms.

What is an algorithm?

An "algorithm" describes a set of steps to solve a problem. For programmers, an algorithm describes the logical structure of a program, including:

- what actions are carried out
- the sequence of the actions.

An algorithm is not written in a particular programming language. Turning an algorithm into a computer program is called coding.

Use of algorithms: Programmers often make algorithms before they begin coding. Why? They use them to:

- set out a plan for how the program will work
- compare different solutions to the problem
- record their solution
- share their solution with other programmers.

Start with output: A programmer works for a client. The programmer finds out what the client needs. This will be the output of the program. Then the programmer writes an algorithm to produce this output, and finally transfers this algorithm into program code.

Flowcharts: A flowchart is a diagram of an algorithm. A flowchart is made of boxes connected by arrows. The boxes stand for actions. The arrows show the flow or sequence of the program

Pseudocode: Pseudocode uses words instead of boxes and arrows. Pseudocode is not exactly like any programming language. It is similar to program code, but you cannot run the code to control the action of the computer.

These are the advantages of using pseudocode compared to flowcharts:

- Pseudocode is similar to normal program code, so program code can easily be written from it.
- It is easier to write a neat, clear version of the algorithm using pseudocode – it does not require special graphics software (like a flowchart would) and pseudocode takes up less space than a flowchart.

There are also disadvantages:

- Pseudocode is more technical than a flowchart.
- Pseudocode can be harder to understand.

Check your readiness

Explain what an algorithm is and how pseudocode and flowcharts are used to prepare algorithms.

8.1 Knowledge test

1. What is an integrated development environment (IDE)?

2. List three features of an IDE.

3. What is an algorithm?

4. Give three reasons why a programmer might write an algorithm.

5. Why might a programmer start by thinking about the output of a program?

6. How does a flowchart show the sequence of actions?

7. How is pseudocode different from any programming language?

8. What are the advantages of pseudocode compared to flowcharts?

8.2 Begin coding

Output

Unlike an algorithm, program code can be executed (run). When you run the code, the processor follows the instructions in the program.

Python

Python is an interpreted language. When you run the code the interpreter reads one Python command at a time. The interpreter works out the machine code instruction that matches the command. The interpreter sends that instruction to the CPU. The CPU carries out the instruction. This will repeat until all the commands have been interpreted.

When your program code is ready you will:

- **save** the code as a file in secondary storage
- **run** the code so the CPU executes the commands.

The output of the program will appear in the "Python Shell" window.

Syntax errors: If you make a syntax error the interpreter cannot convert the code into an instruction. An error message appears in the "Python Shell" window. The error message explains the error so you can fix it.

You can add comments to your code. Comments are ignored by the interpreter. The interpreter will not try to interpret or execute these lines of code. In Python, any line that begins with # is a comment.

Comments are used to:

- set out the structure of a program
- add explanations for a human reader.

Check your readiness

Start up Python and create a program with comments in it. If you do not know any other Python commands then simply add comments. Save and run the program. Fix any syntax errors.

You need to know:
- how to save and run a Python program
- when to use comments
- how to spot syntax errors.

Key terms
Interpreter: a type of translator that turns program code into machine code
Syntax: refers to the rules of a language, such as a programming language
Syntax error: code that breaks the rules of the programming language.

The Python print command produces output. It displays a string on the screen. The print command is a predefined function that comes as part of standard Python code.

Python

Print command: `print` will make Python display a string on the screen. This command will print the string xxx.

```
print("xxx")
```

This command will print a blank line.

```
print("\n")
```

You need to know:
- how to use the print command to produce output
- what a predefined function is.

Function: `print` is a function. A function is a command that transforms a value. The value that is transformed is called the parameter. The parameter of a print command is the string that it prints.

Predefined function: Some functions are made by programmers. Others are predefined. Predefined functions come as part of standard Python. `print` is a predefined function.

IDLE uses colours to show the different types of code in your program:

- function names are purple
- strings are green
- comments are red.

Check your readiness

Write a Python program that prints a message to the user. Write notes on the meaning of the term "function". What is a predefined function?

Sequence

Pseudocode and flowcharts let you set out commands in sequence. The PRINT command and the output box are used for outputs from the algorithm.

Pseudocode

Like programs, algorithms show commands in sequence. Each line is carried out in the order in which it is written.

PRINT: Pseudocode uses a print command similar to Python. It is used to output a string. The string is shown with quote marks. The word PRINT is written in upper case letters. There are no brackets.

Example:

```
PRINT "Welcome to My Snaps"
PRINT "You can upload photos"
PRINT "You can share them with your friends"
```

Flowcharts

Flowchart sequence: Every flowchart has one start and one end. Start and end are shown by boxes with rounded corners. A typical flowchart goes down the page. The sequence of commands is shown by the arrows.

Flowchart output: Outputs are shown using a box like this. Inside the box, write the word 'Output' and the write string to be printed in quote marks.

Output
"Welcome to My Snaps"

Simplify flowcharts: In Pseudocode you write every PRINT command in full. When you make a flowchart you often simplify. Inside an output box, write a summary of the output. This makes the flowchart shorter and easier to read. For example:

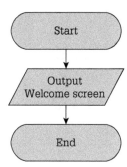

Input

The input command lets the user enter data. The prompt is the message the user will see. Normally, you store user input in a named area of memory called a variable.

Python

Input: The input command is a predefined function in Python. An input command is shown below. Instead of dots, type the prompt that you want the user to see:

```
input ("...")
```

Store input: Usually you want the computer to remember the user input. You can store the user input in a named memory location, which is called a variable.

This command will take the user input and store it as a variable called password:

```
Password = input ("Enter the password")
```

Name variables: You can choose any name for a variable. The name should remind you of what data is stored in that variable. Use only letters, numbers and the underscore character.

You need to know:
- what a variable is
- how to use the input command to input data to the computer
- how to store input as a variable.

Key terms

Input to a program: the data that goes into the computer

Prompt: a message to the user. The prompt tells the user what data to enter.

Declare variables: In some programming languages you have to create a variable with a special command before you can use it. That is called declaring the variable.

In Python you don't have to declare variables with a special command. The computer makes the variable for you when you need it. This is called initialising the variable.

Check your readiness

Enter a command to get user input and store it as a variable called UserName. Include a suitable prompt.

Assign a value

The equals sign is used to assign a value to a variable. You can use the print command to output this value.

You need to know:
- how to assign a value to a variable
- how to output the value stored in a variable.

Python
The equals sign is used to assign a value to a variable.

```
Variable = value
```

For example:

```
UserName = "CyberMaster"

Age = 25
```

Output a variable: You can output a variable using the print command. Don't put quote marks round the name of the variable. The computer will output the value assigned to the variable.

Example:

```
print(Password)
```

Output string plus variable: You can print a string and a variable together. Put a comma inbetween them.

Example:

```
print("Your password is ", Password)
```

Constants: Some programming languages let you use constants as well as variables. The value of a constant is set by the program code. This value cannot change. Constants are not used in Python. Instead, if you needed a constant in your program, you would create a variable, assign a value to the variable, and leave the value unchanged throughout the program.

Check your readiness

Create a Python program that assigns values to variables called FirstName, SecondName and Age. Add a command that prints these values as a single line.

Calculated values

Using arithmetic operators you can get the computer to carry out calculations. The result of the calculation is assigned to a variable.

Python

Calculation: You have learned how to assign a number value to a variable. You can also assign the result of a calculation to a variable.

Example: This Python command will work out 240 + 270 and assign the result to a variable called Cost.

```
Cost = 240 + 270
```

The variable Cost now stores the result of the calculation. You could use the print command to output the value stored in the variable.

Arithmetic operators: The symbols used in calculation are called arithmetic operators. They are:

+ plus

- minus

* multiply

/ divide

You can also do calculations with variables. The computer will use the value stored in the variable.

Example: These Python commands assign a value to two variables, then use the values in another calculation.

```
Cost = 510
Income = 600
Profit = Income - Cost
```

Finally, you can use the name of a variable on both sides of the equals sign. For example, this command will increase the value stored in the variable Age by 1.

```
Age = Age + 1
```

This command will take the value stored in the variable profit, divide it by 2, and store the result.

```
Profit = Profit/2
```

Check your readiness

Write a program that assigns the value 1000 to a variable called Income. Write commands to make income ten times bigger, then print it.

Data types

Every variable has a data type. Input variables are always string data type. Before you use these variables in calculations you must change the data type.

Python

Data types: The computer uses different methods to store different types of data. The different storage methods are called data types. These are some typical data types used in programming:

- Integer – this stores a whole number.
- Float – this stores any number, including fractions and decimals (also called "real" numbers).
- String – this stores any series of text characters.
- Boolean– this stores True or False only.
- Char – short for "character"– this stores a single text character. This variable type is not used in Python.

Choose data type: In some programming languages you have to tell the computer what data type to use. In Python you do not do this. The computer chooses the data type, by looking at the assigned value.

Data type of input values: The computer always uses the string data type for an input value. String data type cannot be used in calculations.

Often programmers want to use user input in calculations.

Change data type: If you want to use an input variable in a calculation you must change the variable from string to a numeric data type. You must change the data type before you use the variable in a calculation.

You could change input data to float, or integer, or data.

This command will convert `Value1` to integer data type:

```
Value1 = int(Value1)
```

This command will change Value2 to the float data type:

```
Value2 = float(Value2)
```

> **Check your readiness**
>
> Write a Python program that inputs the cost of an item, then adds 17 per cent VAT and prints it. To add 17 per cent, to a value, multiply it by 1.17.

Variables in pseudocode

Pseudocode uses very similar commands to Python to work with variables. Variables can be assigned values, can store input, can be used for calculations and can be output.

Pseudocode

Variables in pseudocode: In program code (such as Python) a variable is a named memory location. Pseudocode also includes variables. The variables in pseudocode do not stand for real memory locations. They are just a way of planning the logic of the program. Choose variable names just as you would in any programming language. In pseudocode variables do not have data types.

Input a value: Real programs take user input and store it in a variable. Pseudocode also has this feature. The user input is stored in a variable, just as in other program code. In pseudocode you use the word READ followed by the name of the variable.

```
READ Password
```

Assign a value: In Python you use the equals sign to assign a value to a variable. In pseudocode you use the arrow symbol instead.

```
Password ← "Sesame"
```

Remember the variable name comes first, then the value. You can imagine the arrow sending the value into the variable.

Calculate a value: Pseudocode uses the same arithmetic operators as Python. You can assign a calculated value to a variable, just as in Python.

```
Cost ← 200
Income ← 230
Profit ← Cost - Income
```

Output a value: Pseudocode uses the word PRINT to output a variable.

```
PRINT Profit
```

Check your readiness

Write a pseudocode algorithm that inputs the cost of an item, then adds 17 per cent VAT and prints it. To add 17 per cent, multiply by 1.17.

Variables in flowcharts

Flowcharts can use variables. Variables can be assigned values, can store input, can be used for calculations, and can be output.

You need to know:
- how to draw and understand flowcharts that use variables.

Variables in flowcharts

You can include variables in flowchart algorithms. You can input and output variables. You can assign values to variables and use arithmetic operators. You don't need to worry about data types.

This flowchart shape stands for input and output.

INPUT Variable   OUTPUT Variable

For input: Inside the box put the word INPUT and the name of the variable. You can include more than one variable in each input box.

For output: Use the same shape of box. Inside the box put the word OUTPUT and the name of one or more variables.

Assign a value: To assign a value to a variable, use a rectangular-shaped box.

$$\boxed{\text{Variable = Value}}$$

Inside the box you can use the equals sign as used in Python, or the arrow sign as used in pseudocode. **Remember the general rule:** the name of the variable comes first, then the value.

You can assign the result of a calculation to a variable. Use the normal arithmetic operators. Show the calculation inside the box.

$$\boxed{\text{Variable = A + B}}$$

Check your readiness

Write a flowchart algorithm that inputs the cost of an item, then adds 17 per cent VAT and prints it. To add 17 per cent multiply by 1.17.

8.2 Knowledge test

1. Write a Python program that inputs a decimal number, multiplies it by 100, and prints it as a percentage. Run the program and correct any syntax errors.

2. Write a pseudocode version of the same program.

3. Write a flowchart version of the same program.

8.3 Selection

Logical decision

A logical test uses a relational operator to compare two values. An algorithm can use a logical test to choose between two different actions.

You need to know:
- what a logical test is
- how to use relational operators to make logical tests
- how to draw and understand flowcharts that use logical tests.

Pseudocode

Selection: In some programs the computer must choose between two different actions. This is called selection. The computer uses a logical test to choose between the two actions.

Relational operators: Most logical tests compare two values. To compare two values you use a relational operator. Here are the main relational operators:

= equal to

<> not equal

< less than

> more than

The operators = and <> can be used with any values. The operators > and < can only be used with number values.

Decision box: In a flowchart a logical test goes inside a decision box, which is a diamond shape

One arrow goes into the decision box. Two arrows come out of the decision box. The arrows coming out are labelled YES and NO. The computer chooses either YES or NO based on the logical test.

On the right, you can see an example of a flowchart which contains a decision box. The algorithm inputs a value that is a mark out of 100. If you get more than 59 then you pass the test.

One end: Every algorithm has only one end point. The arrows must join up again before the end.

Key term

Logical test: a test that always gives the answer True or False (and no other answer). Most logical tests compare two values.

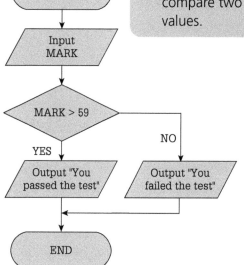

Check your readiness

Draw a flowchart for an algorithm that inputs a password. If the password is "Raven" the message `Welcome to the game` is displayed. If the result of the test is False the message `Password incorrect` is displayed.

Python `if`

Selection in Python is done using an `if` statement. Indentation is used to show the actions that belong within the statement.

You need to know:
- how to write a Python program that includes an `if` statement.

Python

Selection means that the computer can choose different actions: The computer chooses what actions to take, based on a logical test.

Logical tests use relational operators. Python uses the following relational operators:

> `==` equal to
>
> `!=` not equal
>
> `<` less than
>
> `>` more than

The operators > and < can only be used with number values.

An `if` statement has this structure:

> `if test:`

Instead of the word *test* you would enter a logical test. Here are some examples:

> `if Age > 17:`
>
> `if UserName != "Amelia99":`
>
> `if Payment == £49.99:`

Don't forget the colon at the end :

Conditional structure: One or more commands follow the `if` statement. The commands are indented. If the result of the test is True the commands will be carried out. If the result of the test is False the commands will not be carried out.

Indentation shows what lines belong "inside" the conditional structure. If you use IDLE to write Python code, the indentation will be added automatically after the colon :

Stop the indentation to mark the end of the conditional structure.

Here is an example of a Python program that uses a conditional structure.

```
## Evaluate test mark
Mark = input("enter the test mark")
Mark = int(Mark)
if Mark > 59:
    print("you passed the test")
```

Key term
Indentation: space before a line starts.

Check your readiness

Write a Python program that inputs a password. If the password is "Raven" the message `Welcome to the game` is displayed.

Python `if...else...`

An `if` statement can be combined with an `else` statement. The indented lines following `if` are carried out if the result of the test is True. The indented lines following `else` are carried out if the result of the test is false.

You need to know:
- how to write a Python program that includes `if...else`.

Python

In the previous section you wrote a Python program that uses an `if` statement. The `if` statement included a logical test. The lines that followed the `if` statement were indented. The indented lines were carried out if the result of the test was True.

You can now add an extra line to this program.

`else:`

This line is not indented. It does not include a logical test. The lines that follow `else` are indented. These lines will be carried out if the result of the test is False.

Here is an example.

```
## Evaluate test mark
Mark = input("enter the test mark ")
Mark = int(Mark)
if Mark > 59:
    print("you passed the test")
else:
    print("you failed the test")
```

Indentation: Indentation is important. The `if` statement and the `else` statement are not indented. The lines that follow `if` and `else` are indented. The indentation shows the lines that belong "inside" the `if` statement and the `else` statement.

There are several ways to turn indentation on and off:

- IDLE will add indentation automatically after a colon :
- You can use the tab key or press the space bar to add indentation.
- You can select a block of text and turn indent on and off using the format menu.
- You can delete the indentation with the backspace or delete keys.

Check your readiness

Write a Python program that inputs a password. If the password is "Raven" the message Welcome to the game is displayed. If the result of the Test is false the message Password incorrect is displayed.

Python `elif`

Python `if... else...` uses a single logical test that can give the answer True or False. An alternative called `elif` lets you include more than one logical test. The tests do not need to use the same variable, but they often do.

You need to know:
- how to use `elif` to include multiple tests in a Python program.

Python

The `if... else...` structure uses a logical test. The result of a logical test can be True or False.

Python has a more complex structure called `elif`. `elif` lets you use a series of logical tests. This means that the program can select between more than two choices.

You could use `elif` when your program includes a menu of choices for the user. If you want to give the user more than a yes/no choice, you can use `elif`.

You begin the `elif` command with a normal `if` statement. Here is an example.

```
print("you have been given the values 12 and 3")
Choice = input("Enter an arithmetic operator")
if Choice = "+":
    Result = 12 + 3
print("The result is", Result)
```

By using `elif` you can extend the selection. You can add more logical tests. Just type the word `elif` and a logical test. Each `elif` statement uses a different logical test. There can be as many examples of `elif` as you want.

```
print("you have been given the values 12 and 3")
Choice = input("Enter an arithmetic operator")
if Choice = "+":
    Result = 12 + 3
elif Choice = "-":
    Result = 12 - 3
elif Choice = "*":
    Result = 12 * 3
print("The result is", Result)
```

You can also include else at the end of the `elif`. The `else` statement will be carried out if **none** of the test results are True.

Check your readiness

Extend the example given on this page to include the arithmetic operator / and an `else` statement that says "you did not choose a valid arithmetic operator".

Selection in pseudocode

The pseudocode `IF... ELSE... ENDIF` structure is very similar to the Python `if... else` structure and is used in the same way.

You need to know:
* how to write and understand pseudocode algorithms that use `IF` and `ELSE`.

Pseudocode

If you have learned to use `if`, `else` and `elif` in Python you will find it easy to use similar structures in pseudocode. In pseudocode we use these relational operators:

= equal to

<> not equal

< less than

> more than

In pseudocode the `IF` statement begins like this.

```
IF test THEN
```

Here are some examples.

```
IF Age > 17 THEN
IF UserName <> "Amelia99" THEN
IF Payment = £49.99 THEN
```

The `IF` structure ends with the word `ENDIF`. Here is an example.

```
READ MARK
IF Mark > 59 THEN
    PRINT "you passed"
ENDIF
```

Indentation is not as important in pseudocode as in Python. You can include indentation to make the code easier to read but this is not essential. Sometimes the entire `IF.. THEN.. ENDIF` statement can be shown on a single line.

```
IF Mark > 59 THEN PRINT "you passed" ENDIF
```

Else is used in the same way as it is in Python but `ELSE` is in upper case and no colon is needed. Here is an example.

```
READ MARK
IF Mark > 59 THEN
    PRINT "you passed"
ELSE
    PRINT "you failed"
ENDIF
```

Check your readiness

Make a Python program that inputs a password. If the password is "Raven" the message `Welcome to the game` is displayed. If the result of the test is False the message `Password incorrect` is displayed.

The CASE statement is used in pseudocode to create a condition structure that includes a series of tests. All the tests must use the same variable.

You need to know:

- how to write and understand pseudocode algorithms that use CASE.

Pseudocode

In pseudocode a CASE statement lets you use a series of logical tests.

The CASE statement starts with the word CASE, then a variable name, then the word OF.

```
CASE Variable OF
```

The CASE statement includes several comparison values. After each value there is a command. The computer carries out each comparison in turn, as a series of logical tests. When it finds a test that is true it carries out that command.

If none of the tests match the desired value, it carries out the final command, which begins with the word OTHERWISE.

The CASE statement finishes with the word ENDCASE.

Here is an example. It uses a variable called Mark which stores how many marks a student got in a test.

```
CASE Mark OF
    100: PRINT "Grade A"
    >75: PRINT "Grade B"
    >50: PRINT "Grade C"
OTHERWISE
    PRINT "Grade U"
ENDCASE
```

Unlike the Python elif command, all the logical tests in a CASE statement must use the same variable.

Check your readiness

You made a Python program using elif. Convert this to a pseudocode algorithm using CASE.

8.3 Knowledge test

1. Make a Python program that inputs two values and prints the value that is greatest. Run the program and remove any syntax errors.

2. Draw a flowchart algorithm that inputs two values and prints the value that is greatest.

3. Write a pseudocode algorithm that inputs two values and prints the value that is greatest.

4. Make a Python program that inputs one value and tells you if it is a negative number, zero, or a positive number. Use `elif`. Run the program and remove any syntax errors.

5. Write a pseudocode algorithm that inputs one value and tells you if it is a negative number, zero, or a positive number. Use `CASE`.

8.4 Repetition

Loops

> Repetition, or looping, means that a piece of code is repeated. The loop can be stopped by an exit condition. The two types of loop have different exit conditions.

You need to know:
- what repetition is
- what an exit condition is
- the different types of loop
- how to draw and understand a flowchart that has a loop in it.

Flowcharts

A loop is a section of code that is repeated. Every loop must have an exit condition.

The exit condition tells the computer when to stop repeating the loop. If you use a loop in your programs you must make sure that there is an exit condition that can stop the loop.

There are two types of loop. They have different exit conditions:

- In a **counter-controlled** loop, the loop stops after a set number of repetitions.
- In a **condition-controlled** loop, a logical test is used to stop the loop.

A counter-controlled loop uses a variable called the counter. The counter goes up by 1 every time the loop repeats. When the counter reaches a maximum value the loop stops. In Python, a counter-controlled loop is also called a `for` loop.

A condition-controlled loop uses a logical test. The result of the test tells the computer whether to repeat the loop. The loop might repeat once, or a million times. In Python a condition-controlled loop is also called a `while` loop.

In a flowchart the exit condition is shown using a decision box. It is most common to show the decision box at the end of the loop because of the way flowcharts are structured.

If the result of the test is False, the arrow goes up the flowchart to the start of the loop.

If the result of the test is True, the arrow goes down to the end of the flowchart, and the loop stops.

The example on the right asks a mathematics question and checks the user's answer.

Key terms
Increment: to increase a value by one
Iteration: one repetition of a loop.

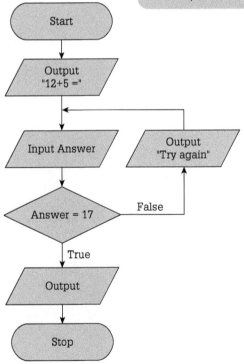

Check your readiness

Draw a flowchart algorithm for a program that asks for a four-digit pass code and loops until the correct code is entered.

`for` loops

Python includes a counter-controlled loop called a `for` loop. A `for` loop uses a counter variable. The counter variable counts from a start to a stop value.

Python

Counter variable: A counter-controlled loop uses a variable as the counter. You can choose any name for the counter variable. Many programmers choose the single letter `i`. The counter variable will count from a minimum to a maximum value.

Python for loop: In Python a counter-controlled loop is called a `for` loop. Here are some examples of `for` loops. In each case the counter is called `i`.

```
for i in range (1, 100):
for i in range (0, 5):
for i in range (4, 8):
```

The two numbers in brackets are the start and stop values for the counter. If you do not specify a start value, Python will start at 0. Python will stop just before it reaches the stop value. The start and stop values must be integers.

The first line is followed by one or more indented lines. Indentation shows the lines that belong inside the loop. The indented lines will be repeated. IDLE will add indentation automatically after the colon.

This Python program will print the 8 times table.

```
for i in range (1, 13):
    print(i, " x 8 = ", i*8)
```

This Python program will count up to a maximum value.

```
max = input("enter the maximum value")
max = int(max)
for i in range (max+1):
    print(i)
```

If the stop value is smaller than the start value, Python will count backwards.

Check your readiness

2^2 means 2*2.
2^3 means 2*2*2.
Write a program in Python that will input a number n and then show the value of 2^n.

`while` loops

Python includes a condition-controlled loop called a `while` loop. A `while` loop includes a logical test. The loop will stop when the logical test is false.

Python

In Python, a condition-controlled loop is called a `while` loop. A `while` loop starts with a logical test. With every iteration of the loop, the computer will repeat the logical test.

Here are some examples of the first lines of different `while` loops.

```
while Password != "Raven":
while Cost == 99.00:
while Age < 18:
```

Each of these examples includes a logical test. The loop will repeat while the result of the test is True. The loop will stop when the result of the test is False.

The lines that follow the first line will be indented. The indented lines belong "inside" the loop. These lines will be repeated.

The logical test has a variable in it.

You must include a line before the loop that sets the value of this variable. This means that you can start the loop.

You must include a line inside the loop that changes the value of this variable. This means that you can stop the loop.

Here is an example of a `while` loop. It will repeat until the user guesses the right number.

```
guess = 0
while guess != 7:
    guess = input("guess the number:")
    guess = int(guess)
print("You guessed it!")
```

Check your readiness

Write a Python program that asks a general knowledge question and repeats until the user enters the right answer. You can choose any question you want.

Loops in pseudocode

Pseudocode has FOR loops and WHILE loops that are similar to loops in Python.

You need to know:
- how to write a pseudocode algorithm that uses a FOR loop or a WHILE loop.

Pseudocode

If you understand `for` and `while` loops in Python it is easy to use the same types of loop in pseudocode algorithms.

In pseudocode the command words are shown in upper case. Indentation is used for neatness, but it is less important in pseudocode than in Python.

Here is an example of a FOR loop. It matches an example you have already seen in Python.

```
FOR i ← 1 TO 12
    PRINT i*8
NEXT i
```

Be aware of differences between pseudocode and Python. In pseudocode:
- an arrow is used to show the range from start to stop value
- the structure ends with NEXT i
- the loop stops **after** it reaches the stop value.

Here is an example of an algorithm with a WHILE loop. It matches another example you've already seen on Python.

```
GUESS ← 0
WHILE guess <> 7 DO
      READ guess
ENDWHILE
PRINT "You guessed it!"
```

Here, pseudocode differs from Python in that:
- The word DO is used instead of the colon.
- The structure ends with the word ENDWHILE.

Check your readiness

Write pseudocode algorithms to match any Python programs you have written that use for and while loops. Practise several examples.

Pseudocode includes an extra type of loop, called a REPEAT loop. It is a condition-controlled loop, but the test is at the bottom of the loop.

You need to know:
- how to write pseudocode algorithms that use REPEAT loops.

Pseudocode

A REPEAT... UNTIL loop is a condition-controlled loop. It has different rules from a WHILE loop:
- The test comes at the end of the loop.
- The loop stops when the result of the test is True.

Here is an example of an algorithm using a REPEAT loop.

```
REPEAT
      READ guess
UNTIL guess = 7
PRINT "You guessed it!"
```

The test comes at the bottom of the loop. Algorithms that use a REPEAT loop may be shorter and easier to understand than algorithms that use a WHILE loop. The REPEAT loop works differently from the WHILE loop, so there are differences to the structure of the algorithm:
- You do not have to set the value of the test variable before the loop starts.
- The commands inside the loop come before the test.
- The commands inside the loop are carried out at least once, no matter what the test result.

In a flowchart the test comes at the bottom of the loop. That means a REPEAT loop matches the structure of a typical flowchart loop.

Check your readiness

Write a Python program that asks a general knowledge question and repeats until the user enters the right answer. You can choose any question you want. Use a REPEAT loop.

8.4 Knowledge test

A factorial is a mathematical term. It is shown by an exclamation mark. For example, 4! means "4 factorial". To calculate the factorial of a number, multiply together all the numbers from 1 up to that number.

Here are some examples:

$$2! = 1*2 = 2$$
$$4! = 1*2*3*4 = 24$$
$$6! = 1*2*3*4*5*6 = 720$$

1. Write a Python program that inputs a number and calculates the factorial of that number. Use a for loop.

2. Write a pseudocode version of the factorial program using the FOR loop.

3. Draw a flowchart to match the factorial program.

4. Write a Python program that uses a while loop to simulate the following scenario:
   Step 1 The user inputs an email address.
   Step 2 The program asks the user to input the email address a second time.
   Step 3 If the second version matches the first, the program stops.
   Step 4 If the second version does not match the first, the program loops and asks for the email address again.

5. Write a pseudocode version of the email address program from question **4**. Use a WHILE loop.

6. Write a pseudocode version of the email address program from question **4**. Use a REPEAT loop.

7. Draw a flowchart to match the email address program from question **4**.

8.5 Data structures

Lists and arrays

A list is a Python data structure made up of a series of connected variables called elements. Each element is identified by an index number. The list is enclosed in square brackets.

You need to know:
- the meaning of "list", "element" and "index number"
- how to write a Python program that stores data in a list.

Python

A list is made of elements. Here is an example of a Python command that creates a list with three elements.

```
Science = ["Physics", "Chemistry", "Biology"]
```

The elements are separated by commas. The whole list is enclosed in square brackets.

Each element in a list has its own name. The name of an element is the name of the list plus an index number. The first element in the list is:

```
Science[0]
```

The next is:

```
Science[1]
```

You can print the whole list with this command:

```
print(Science)
```

You can print a single list element with a command like this:

```
print(Science[1])
```

You can assign the value of an element to another variable:

```
MyCourse = Science[1]
```

You can use a list variable in logical tests:

```
if Science[1] == "Botany":
```

Key terms

List: a series of connected memory locations with an overall name, which can store several values in a series

Element: the name of each value in a list

Index number: each element in the list is named after the list name plus a number, called the index number.

Check your readiness

Write a Python program that creates a list of five bird species. Add a command to print the whole list. Print the elements of the list one at a time using five different commands.

Output a list

In Python, `for` loops are ideal for working with lists. Using a `for` loop, you can print each element in the list one by one.

You need to know:
- how to use a `for` loop to print the elements of a list.

Python

A Python program can print all the elements in a list one by one. It uses a counter-controlled loop (a `for` loop). This method can print a list of any size.

A `for` loop uses a counter variable. The counter variable is typically the letter `i`. When we print a list the variable `i` has a double use:

- It is the counter variable of the `for` loop.
- It is the index number for the list.

Every counter-controlled loop needs a start and stop value. This is the process when we count through a list:

- The first element on the list is index number 0, so the start value is 0.
- We want the loop to stop when we reach the end of the list, so the stop value is the length of the list.

How do we know when to stop? The `len()` function counts how many elements there are in a list. The following command counts how many elements there are in the list called `Science`. It stores the value in a variable called `Listlength`.

```
ListLength = len(Science)
```

Now we can use the variable `ListLength` as the stop value of the counter-controlled loop.

Here is the first line of the loop:

```
for i in range (ListLength):
```

The counter will increment from 0, up to the length of the list. Here is the complete program.

```
Science = ["Physics", "Chemistry", "Biology"]
ListLength = len(Science)
for i in range (ListLength):
    print(Science[i])
```

Check your readiness

You wrote a Python program that creates a list of five bird species. Add a command to print the elements of the list one at a time. Use a `for` loop.

Add elements to a list

You have learned to make a whole list with a single command. You can also add and remove elements from a list one at a time.

Python

You can make a list with no elements in it. This command makes an empty list called `Rainbow`:

```
Rainbow = []
```

Next you can add elements to this empty list. Adding an element to a list is called appending. For example, this command will add the element `Green` to the list `Rainbow`.

```
Rainbow.append("Green")
```

A command like this will add one element to a list.

You need to know:

- how to write a Python program that builds up a list by adding elements to it.

Key term

Append: add to the end; appending a value to a list makes the list longer.

You can also get user input, and add that to the list.

```
NewColour = input("Add a new colour to the list")
Rainbow.append(NewColour)
```

If you want the user to add many elements it is best to use a loop. If you know how many elements you need to add to the list you can use a counter-controlled loop. This example adds five elements.

```
Rainbow = []
for i in range(5):
    NewColour = input("Add a new colour")
    Rainbow.append(NewColour)
```

If you don't know how many elements you need to add, use a condition-controlled loop.

```
Rainbow = []
Continue = "Y"
while Continue == "Y":
    NewColour = input("Add a new colour")
    Rainbow.append(NewColour)
    Continue = input ("Add another? (Y/N)")
```

Check your readiness
Write a Python program that creates an empty list of bird species. Add a for `loop` that lets the user add five elements to the list. Add a `for` loop that prints the five elements.

Arrays in pseudocode

Pseudocode has a structure called an array which is very similar to a list. You can use a `for` loop to add elements to an array, and to print an array.

Pseudocode
You have learned about lists in Python. Pseudocode and most other programming languages do not use lists. Instead they have structures called arrays. An array is similar to a list. From the point of view of this course you can use arrays and lists in exactly the same way.

Making an array is called declaring the array. To declare an empty array in pseudocode you should specify the number of elements in the array. This command makes a list with 30 elements, starting at 1.

```
StudentName[1:30]
```

You need to know:
- that an array is very similar to a list
- how to write pseudocode algorithms to work with arrays.

Key terms

Array: a similar data structure to a list. Arrays are used in pseudocode and many other programming languages.

You can use a for loop to count through the 30 elements and add a value to each one.

```
FOR i ← 1 TO 30
    INPUT Name
    StudentName[i] ← Name
Next i
```

You can use a for loop to count through the 30 elements and print each one.

```
FOR i ← 1 TO 30
    PRINT StudentName[i]
Next i
```

Key term
Declare: Making an empty array is called declaring the array.

Check your readiness

Write a pseudocode algorithm that declares an array called `BirdSpecies` with five elements. Add a `for` loop that lets the user set the value of the five elements of the array. Add a `for` loop that prints the five elements.

8.5 Knowledge test

A doctor wants to store the names of a small selection of her patients as a list. You will write a program to help her. In real life a doctor would have hundreds of patients. You will write a program to work with a list of just seven patients.

1. Write a Python program that makes an empty list and then lets the doctor add seven names to the list.

2. Add a command to the program in question **1** to print the seven names on the list.

3. Write a pseudocode algorithm to declare an array of seven names. Enter seven names to the array and print the seven names.

4. Write a Python program that lets the doctor add as many names as she wants to the list. Use a `while` loop. Then add commands to print the list. Use a `for` loop.

Exam preparation

1. Use the information contained in topic 8.1 to describe the meaning of the following terms:
   a IDE
   b Algorithm
   c Flowchart
   d Pseudocode.

Exam-style questions

1. Using pseudocode, write a procedure that will do the following:
   Step 1 Ask you to enter a new password.
   Step 2 Input a new password.
   Step 3 Ask you to re-enter the password.
   Step 4 Input the re-entered password.
   Step 5 Check that the two passwords are the same.
   Step 6 If necessary, repeat the procedure until the two entries are the same.
   Step 7 Output the confirmed password.

2. A list of possible data inputs is shown. State the program data type you would use for each one:

Data Entered	Data Type
25.00	
Smithson	
Yes	
100	
X	

9 Solution development

This page summarises what you will learn about developing solutions to problems. Tick the boxes on this page when you are confident you have learned each item.

9.1 Worked examples

TICK WHEN YOU HAVE LEARNED:

- [ ] how to create an algorithm to count a series
- [ ] how to create an algorithm to add up a total
- [ ] how to create an algorithm to calculate an average
- [ ] how to create an algorithm to carry out verification
- [ ] how to create an algorithm to carry out validation.

9.2 Testing and evaluation

TICK WHEN YOU HAVE LEARNED:

- [ ] why it is important to test software
- [ ] what effective software is
- [ ] how we choose good test data
- [ ] what normal, extreme and abnormal test data are
- [ ] how to record test results
- [ ] how to analyse test results
- [ ] how to use test results to evaluate software.

9.3 Developing algorithms

TICK WHEN YOU HAVE LEARNED:

- [ ] what a trace table is
- [ ] how to make a trace table to test a pseudocode algorithm
- [ ] how to make a trace table to test a flowchart algorithm
- [ ] how to analyse an algorithm to understand its purpose
- [ ] how to find and correct errors in algorithms
- [ ] the different types of error
- [ ] how to make a new algorithm for a given purpose.

9.4 Development methods

TICK WHEN YOU HAVE LEARNED:

- [ ] what top-down programming is
- [ ] the advantages of top-down programming
- [ ] how a system is broken down into sub-systems
- [ ] how to read, understand and draw structure diagrams
- [ ] what subroutines are
- [ ] what predefined functions are
- [ ] what a module is
- [ ] what a code library is.

9.1 Worked examples

Count how many

To count up through a series you use a condition-controlled loop. A variable stores the count. At the start the variable has the value zero. Add 1 to the value of the variable each time the loop repeats.

You need to know:

- how to make an algorithm that counts how many items there are in a series.

Fact check

Basic structure: A program with a condition-controlled loop can be used to count a series. Here is the basic structure.

Before the loop:

- Create a variable called Count. Value is 0.
- Create a variable called Continue. Value is "Y".

Inside the loop:

- Start a condition-controlled loop. It will loop while Continue = "Y".
- If the user types "Y" the loop repeats.
- The value of the variable Count goes up by 1 with each loop.
- If the user types "N" the loop stops.

After the loop:

- After the loop stops, print the value of Count.

Pseudocode

Here is the above program shown as pseudocode. This example uses a WHILE loop. The test is at the top of the loop.

```
Count ← 0
Continue ← "Y"
WHILE Continue = "Y" DO
    Count ← Count + 1
    READ Continue
ENDWHILE
PRINT Count
```

You can also solve this problem using the REPEAT loop, where the test is at the bottom of the loop.

```
Count ← 0
REPEAT
    Count ← Count + 1
    READ Continue
UNTIL Continue <> "Y"
PRINT Count
```

Check your readiness

Write a Python program that matches the algorithm shown on this page. Use a WHILE loop.

Calculate a total

To add up a total you can use a condition-controlled loop or a counter-controlled loop. A variable is used to store the total. At the start this variable has value zero. Each time the loop repeats, the user enters a value. The value is added to the total.

Fact check

Condition-controlled or counter-controlled loop: For this task you can use a condition-controlled loop or a counter-controlled loop. Which one you use depends on whether you know the number of values:

- If you know how many values there are, use a counter-controlled loop.
- If you do not know how many values there are, use a condition-controlled loop.

Follow these steps:

- Create a variable called Sum with value 0.
- Make a loop (either a counter-controlled or condition-controlled loop).
- Every time the loop increments, the user enters a value. The input value is added to the variable Sum.
- When the loop stops, the value of Sum is printed out.

Key term
Sum: the total from adding up a series of numbers.

Pseudocode

Here is a pseudocode algorithm that adds up 12 numbers using the FOR loop.

```
Sum ← 0
FOR i ← 1 TO 12
    READ Number
    Sum ← Sum + Number
NEXT i
```

Below is a pseudocode algorithm that adds up a series of numbers using a WHILE loop.

```
Sum ← 0
Continue ← "Y"
WHILE Continue = "Y" DO
    READ Number
    Sum ← Sum + Number
    READ Continue
ENDWHILE
PRINT Count
```

Check your readiness

Write a Python program that adds up a total. Use a FOR loop.

Write an algorithm in pseudocode to add up a total. Use a REPEAT loop.

Calculate an average

You have learned how to make a loop that counts how many. You have learned to make a loop that adds up a total. Combine both commands into one loop. When the loop is finished, divide the total by the count.

You need to know:
- how to make an algorithm that calculates the average of a series of values.

Fact check

Calculate the mean:

- Count how many values there are (the count).
- Add up the total of the values (the sum).
- Divide the sum by the count to give the average.

The way you do this depends on whether you know how many values there are.

You may know the number of values to add together. Use this number as the stop value of a counter-controlled loop. Use the loop to add up the total. Divide the total by the number of values.

You may not know the number of values to add together. Your program should have a condition-controlled loop. Use the loop to add up a total and also count how many. You have already learned how to do both of these. When the loop is finished, divide the total by the count.

Key term

Mean: an average calculated by dividing the total sum of a series of values by the number of values.

Pseudocode

This algorithm uses a condition-controlled loop to calculate an average.

```
Count ← 0
Sum ← 0
Continue ← "Y"
WHILE Continue = "Y" DO
    Count ← Count + 1
    READ Number
    Sum ← Sum + Number
    READ Continue
ENDWHILE
Average = Sum/Count
PRINT Average
```

Check your readiness

Write a pseudocode algorithm to calculate an average using a counter-controlled loop.

Write a Python program to calculate an average using a condition-controlled loop.

Write an algorithm in pseudocode to calculate an average using a REPEAT loop.

Verification

Errors in data input will produce incorrect output from a program. For this reason, data is checked for errors. The two main methods are verification and validation.

Fact check

Error checks: A program will go wrong if the user enters the wrong data. Many programs include input checks. Input checks work like this:

1. Input from the user is stored in a temporary variable.
2. The program checks the temporary variable.
3. If the variable passes the error check, the value assigned to that variable is used in the program.
4. If the variable fails the error check, the value assigned to that variable is not used in the program.

Error messages: If the data does not pass the error check, the user should see an error message. The error message tells the user what is wrong.

Selection or repetition: You can use an `if` structure (selection) or a loop structure (repetition) for an error check.

Using a loop structure has an advantage and a disadvantage:

- Advantage of loop structure: users have lots of chances to enter the data until they get it right.
- Disadvantage of a loop structure: if users cannot enter the right value, they might get stuck in an endless loop.

Always plan what your program will do if the data does not pass the error check.

> ### Check your readiness
>
> Explain the main features of error checks. Note the purpose of each feature. Explain the difference between using selection and repetition for error checks.

Verification is a way of checking for input errors. With verification, the user must input a value twice. The two inputted values should match. In programming, an `IF` structure or a condition-controlled loop can be used for verification.

Fact check

Verification: This means entering data twice. The two versions are stored as two different variables. The computer will check that the two variables match. Verification is often used to check a new password when you first enter it.

There are two ways to carry out verification. You can use selection (`if...else...`) or repetition (a loop).

Below is an example of a verification algorithm. It uses selection. The user must enter a password twice. In this example the two attempts are called `Try1` and `Try2`. If the two values match, this value is assigned as the password. If they do not match, an error message is shown.

```
READ Try1
READ Try2
IF Try1 = Try2 THEN
    Password ← Try1
ELSE
    PRINT "The two versions did not match"
ENDIF
```

Here is another example of a verification algorithm. It uses a condition-controlled loop. If `Try1` and `Try2` do not match, then the loop repeats.

```
READ Try1
READ Try2
WHILE Try1 <> Try2 DO
    PRINT "The two versions did not match"
    READ Try1
    READ Try2
ENDWHILE
Password ← Try1
```

Check your readiness

Write a Python program that verifies a password using selection.

Write a Python program that verifies a password using repetition.

Write a verification algorithm that uses a REPEAT loop.

Validation

Validation is a way of checking for input errors. The input value is checked against one or more rules called the validation criteria. In programming an IF structure, a CASE structure or a condition-controlled loop can be used for validation.

You need to know:
- how to design algorithms that include input validation.

Fact check

Validation: This is a way to check that the user has entered data of the right general type. An input variable is checked against validation criteria. If data does not match the validation criteria it is not used in the program.

Here are some examples of validation criteria:

- Range check – a number variable is within minimum and maximum allowed values.
- Length check – a text variable contains the right number of characters.
- Type check – a variable is the right data type.

Key term
Validation criteria: rules about what input can be accepted by the program.
Note: The singular of "criteria" is "criterion".

- Presence check – a value has been entered (that is, the variable cannot be left empty).

Any of these criteria can be turned into a logical test. The test can be used in selection or repetition.

Validation can use repetition. A condition-controlled loop is used. The loop will repeat until the user enters data that matches the criteria. You can use a WHILE loop or a REPEAT loop.

Validation can use selection. If there is only one validation criterion, you can use IF... ELSE. If there are many validation criteria, you can use CASE. In Python programs, elif is used instead of CASE.

Check your readiness

A program requires validation of age. The age must be a number greater than 0. Write a pseudocode algorithm that uses IF... ELSE to validate the age. Write a Python program that does the same thing.

Validation algorithms

You will look at examples of algorithms that carry out validation.

You need to know:
- how to make an algorithm to perform input validation.

Fact check

There are many different validation algorithms.

This validation algorithm uses a WHILE loop. If the user enters a number above 99 then the loop will repeat. If the first number entered is less than 99, the algorithm will not need to perform the loop at all.

```
READ Number
WHILE Number > 99 DO
    PRINT "The number is too big"
    READ Number
ENDWHILE
```

The validation algorithm below uses CASE. It checks that the number is not above 99 and that the number is not below 0.

```
READ Number
CASE Number OF
    >99: PRINT "The number is too big"
    <0: PRINT "The number is too small"
OTHERWISE
    PRINT "Number is valid"
ENDCASE
```

This Python program checks the length of a password. The password must be at least eight characters long.

```python
Password = input("enter a password:")
Length = len(Password)
while Length < 8:
    print("Must be at least 8 characters")
    Password = input("enter a password:")
    Length = len(Password)
print("Password accepted")
```

Check your readiness

Write a Python program that uses `elif` to check that a password is not bigger than 15 characters or smaller than 8 characters.

Write a pseudocode algorithm that checks that a number is smaller than 0. Use a loop structure.

9.1 Knowledge test

1. What does this pseudocode algorithm do?

```
A ← 0
B ← "X"
WHILE B = "X" DO
    A ← A + 1
    READ B
ENDWHILE
PRINT A
```

2. What does this pseudocode algorithm do?

```
A ← 0
READ B
FOR i ← 1 TO B
    READ C
    A ← A + C
NEXT i
PRINT A
```

3. A student takes five exams. Write a pseudocode algorithm that calculates his average mark.

4. A social media site asks you to enter your email address when you join. Write a pseudocode algorithm that uses a REPEAT loop to verify the email address.

5. A website asks for your day, month and year of birth. These are stored as three different variables. Write a Python program that carries out one validation check on one of these variables. You can use any program structure you like.

Extension work

Write a longer Python program that carries out a wide range of error checks on the day, month and year variables.

9.2 Testing and evaluation

Test data

A program must be tested before it is given to the client. You test a program by entering test data, and seeing what the output is. Then you compare the output to what the client expects.

You need to know:
- how to test a program
- how to pick suitable test data.

Fact check

Testing software: Programmers must make software that produces the right output for the client. Before software is passed to the client it must be tested. This is how to test software:

- Try out different inputs to the software. The inputs are the test data.
- Check what outputs you get. The outputs are the test results.

The output you get in each case should match the output the client wants.

Programmers will plan, then carry out, a whole series of tests to check that the software they write is functioning properly. They record the test data and the test results. They compare the test results to the expected results:

- If the test results match the expected results: the software has passed the test.
- If the test results do not match expected results: the software has failed the test. The programmer must fix the software.

To carry out a full range of tests you must try inputting many different types of test data. When testing software, programmers test the following types of data:

- **Normal data**. You enter the normal input that you would expect users to enter when they use the software in real life. This test will make sure that the software works as expected in normal everyday use.
- **Extreme data**. You enter large or small numbers that are at the limits of the possible range. The program should accept these inputs. This test will test the limits of the program.
- **Abnormal data**. You enter data that should not be entered by the user. We use these tests because users sometimes make mistakes. This test checks how the program responds when users make these mistakes.

Check your readiness

A programmer made a program where the user must enter day, month and year of birth. What tests would you do on this program?

Evaluation

Good software is effective. When you carry out tests you must record the results. By analysing the results you can decide whether your software is effective.

You need to know:
- how to record and analyse test results to find out if a program is effective.

Fact check

Effective programs: Programmers need to decide whether each program they have made is effective. A program is effective if it:

- produces all the client's requirements
- produces outputs with no errors in them
- works in a way the client likes.

If the program is effective, the programmer can hand the software to the client. If the program is not effective, the programmer must make improvements.

Key term

Effective: something that produces the right effects; the **effects** of a program are its outputs.

Evaluating effectiveness: After the program is completed it is tested. Testing checks the outputs of the program. Analysis compares the outputs of the program to the expected outputs. The actual outputs should match the expected outputs.

The test plan is set out in a table with these columns. The table has one row for every test.

Test number	Purpose of test	Test data	Expected output	Actual result	Analysis

By looking at the test results the programmer can answer these questions:

- Does the software produce the results the client wants?
- Does the software produce the correct outputs with extreme data?
- Does the software work or break down if erroneous data is entered?

Check your readiness

Carry out at least three tests on a piece of software you have made and record the results in a table. If the test used abnormal data input, then what output is expected?

9.2 Knowledge test

A bank developed software to run its cash machines. Here is an example of a screen people see when they use the machine. You have the job of testing this screen.

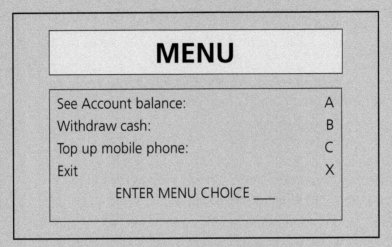

MENU

See Account balance:	A
Withdraw cash:	B
Top up mobile phone:	C
Exit	X

ENTER MENU CHOICE ___

1. Give an example of normal test data you might use. What would you expect to see on the screen after entering this data?

2. Give an example of abnormal test data you might use. What would you expect to see on the screen after entering this data?

3. If a user decides to withdraw cash a box appears like the one below. Give three examples of test data you might enter into this screen.

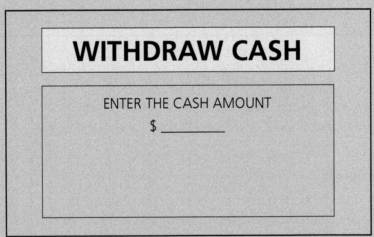

WITHDRAW CASH

ENTER THE CASH AMOUNT

$ _____

4. Make a test table that shows the three tests you planned for question 3. Show the results you would expect to see if the software was effective.

5. Every user is expected to enter a four-digit passcode to log on to the system. The software tester entered three letters. The software logged the tester in to the system. What is your analysis of this test result? Add this test result to the test table.

9.3 Developing algorithms

Trace tables

A trace table is used to test an algorithm. A trace table has a column for every variable in the algorithm. It has a row for every line of the algorithm. The trace table will show you what the algorithm does.

Fact check

Purpose of a trace table: An algorithm sets out the logic of a program. You should test the algorithm before you make the program, but you cannot run it to see what it does. Instead we use a trace table. A trace table traces the values of each variable in an algorithm.

Structure of a trace table: The table has:
- a column for each variable in the algorithm
- a row for each line of the algorithm.

Making a trace table: When you make a trace table, start by numbering every line of the algorithm. You go through an algorithm line by line. You record the value of each variable at every line.

Begin by numbering every line of the algorithm.

```
1    READ A
2    READ B
3    IF A > B THEN
4        READ C
5          A ← A + C
6    ELSE
7          A ← A + B
8    ENDIF
9    PRINT A
```

There are three variables in this algorithm (A, B, and C). We will use the test values 10, 9 and 99. Here is the completed trace table.

Line	A	B	C
1	10		
2	10	9	
3	10	9	
4	10	9	99
5	109	9	99
9	109	9	99

When using these test values, the program does not perform lines 6, 7 and 8 because the IF statement in line 3 was true. Hence, lines 6, 7 and 8 do not appear in the trace table. In line 9 the variable A is output. It has the value 109.

Check your readiness

Complete the trace table using the test values 99 and 150. What is the output?

Trace tables (loops)

> You can make a trace table for an algorithm with a loop. You must repeat some of the lines in the trace table.

You need to know:

• how to make trace tables for algorithms that include repetition.

Fact check

If an algorithm has a loop in it then you may have to go back to previous lines. There is a danger that the trace table will get very long. To prevent that, only show lines where the value of a variable changes.

This algorithm has a counter-controlled FOR loop. The counter value i increments with every loop.

```
1     A ← 0
2     READ B
3     FOR i ← 1 TO B
4         READ C
5         A ← A + C
6     NEXT i
7     PRINT A
```

There are four variables in this algorithm (A, B, C and i). To test the algorithm we will enter the test data B = 2, C = 12 and C = 14.

There are seven lines in this algorithm. The algorithm has a loop in it, so some lines will be repeated.

Line	A	B	i	C
1	0			
2	0	2		
3	0	2	1	
4	0	2	1	12
5	12	2	1	12
6	12	2	2	12
4	12	2	2	14
5	26	2	2	14
6	26	2	3	14

When the value of i reaches 3 the loop stops. Line 7 prints out the value of A. This is 26. Therefore 26 is the output of the algorithm.

Check your readiness

Complete the trace table using the input values 3, 99, 100 and 1. What is the output?

Trace tables (flowcharts)

You can make a trace table for a flowchart. Number the boxes in the flowchart. The table has a column for each variable. It has a row for each box in the flowchart. Show the value of each variable as it changes in each box.

You need to know:
- how to make trace tables to evaluate flowchart algorithms.

Fact check

Example flowchart: Every box in the flowchart is numbered.

There are three variables in this flowchart. These will become columns of the table.

- Sum
- Number
- Continue.

Look for boxes where the value of a variable changes. Each of these becomes a line of the trace table.

We will use this test data:

```
Number = 100
Continue = Y
Number = -99
Continue = N
```

The trace table begins like this.

Box	Sum	Number	Continue
1	0		
2	0	100	
3	100	100	
4	100	100	Y

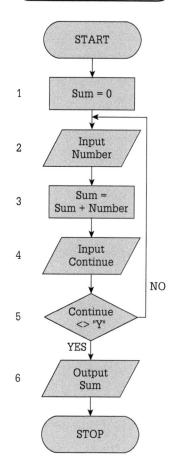

We have got to Box 5. Box 5 is a decision box. A decision box holds a test. The test is:

```
Continue <> "Y"
```

Remember <> means "not the same as". This result of test is False, so we take the NO arrow out of the decision. That takes us to above Box 2. The next input value is -99. The rest of the trace table looks like this.

Box	Sum	Number	Continue
2	100	-99	Y
3	1	-99	Y
4	1	-99	N

Box 5 is a test. The result of the test is True so the loop stops. Box 6 outputs the value of Sum. The value is 1.

Check your readiness

Complete a trace table for the flowchart you made that calculates the factorial for any integer entered by the user (question 3 in 8.4 Knowledge test).

Analyse algorithms

There are strategies you can use to work out what an algorithm does. You find out the result of the algorithm. From the result you can work out the purpose.

You need to know:
- how to work out the result of an algorithm
- how to work out the purpose of an algorithm.

Fact check

Purpose of an algorithm: Its purpose is to produce the result from the given data. To describe the purpose of an algorithm you must describe the relationship between input and output values.

Here are some strategies you can use to work out the purpose of an algorithm:

- Spot familiar algorithms – compare the algorithm to ones you already know such as Count, Total and Average.
- Reflect on variable names – the names of the variables may tell you their purpose (e.g. Count).
- Notice what calculations are used – look at the arithmetic operators used. What calculations are used in this algorithm?
- Notice the structure of the algorithm: Look for selection (if) and repetition (loops).

If there is an IF structure in the algorithm, identify the following:

- What is the logical test?
- What actions are carried out if the test result is True?
- What actions are carried out if the test result is False?

If there is a loop in the algorithm, identify the following:

- Is it a counter-controlled or a condition-controlled loop?
- What actions are carried out inside the loop?
- What is the exit condition of the loop?

Finally, you can choose test data and make a trace table. You may have to run several tests, producing several different trace tables. This is the most time-consuming strategy.

Check your readiness

You have made trace tables for pseudocode and flowchart algorithms. Write an analysis of each of these algorithms.

Find errors in algorithms

The three types of error are syntax, run-time and logical errors. You must use different methods to find and correct each type of error.

You need to know:
- how to find errors in algorithms
- how to correct errors in algorithms.

Fact check

Types of error: There are three types of error that occur in an algorithm or computer program:

- syntax errors
- run-time errors
- logical errors.

Syntax errors: "Syntax" means the rules of a language. That includes the rules of pseudocode. The lines of pseudocode must match the rules of the language. If you get the language wrong, that is a syntax error. Remember these points:

- To spot syntax errors you have to learn the rules of the language.
- To fix syntax errors you must retype the line to match the rules of the language.

Run-time errors: These errors do not break the rules of the language, but when you run the algorithm it may go wrong. There are three common run-time errors:

- a loop without an exit condition
- a division sum that uses a variable with the value 0
- the user inputs data of the wrong data type (e.g. a character string used in a calculation).

Logical errors: A logical error means the algorithm works, but it gives the wrong result. For example, it carries out the wrong calculation. The "wrong" result means it does not match what the client wants. This is what you do to find and fix logical errors:

- Carry out tests.
- Compare the results of the tests with what the client wants.
- If there are logical errors, change the program so it produces different outputs.

Check your readiness

Find the errors in the algorithm shown below. Produce a corrected version of the algorithm.

```
A ← 0
C ← "Y"
WHILE C = "Y" DO
    A ← A + 1
    READ D
    B ← B + D
AVERAGE = A/B
PRINT AVERAGE
```

Create an algorithm

To make an algorithm you must be clear about the required outputs. Then "plan backwards" from these. Ask: What processing will turn user inputs into the outputs the client needs?

Fact check

If you need an algorithm you might be able to reuse an algorithm you already know. You might be able to use it with small changes. Or you may be able to use an algorithm made by another programmer.

Sometimes you need to make an algorithm for a new purpose. Before you start, you should make a plan.

Plan backwards from the outputs. An algorithm processes inputs to create outputs. To plan an algorithm, first identify the outputs you need. Work out what processes will generate those outputs. Work out what inputs you need for those processes to occur.

Your plan should state:

- what values will be input
- what calculations and other processes will occur
- what output will be produced.

You can use the plan to make an algorithm:

- Add READ lines at the start to get inputs
- Add PRINT lines at the end to show outputs
- Place the calculations in between the inputs and the outputs.

To develop your algorithm fully, think about:

- what arithmetic operators you will need
- whether you need to use IF structures
- whether you need to use loops
- the logical tests you will use.

After you've written an algorithm, use the methods you have already learned to find and remove any errors. Use the trace table method to test the algorithm and check the results it produces.

Check your readiness

Make an algorithm where the user inputs two numbers and the program tells the user what percentage the first number is of the second number. Test the algorithm using a trace table.

9.3 Knowledge test

1. Fill in the gaps in this statement.
   A trace table is used to test and _____ an algorithm. A trace table has a column for each _____ in the algorithm. Before making a trace table you should number every _____ of a pseudocode algorithm and every _____ of a flowchart. To simplify a trace table, only include rows where a _____ changes value.

2. Here is a pseudocode algorithm. The lines are numbered.
   ```
   1  A ← 0

   2  B ← "Y"

   3  WHILE B = "Y"

   4     READ C

   5     IF C > A THEN A ← C ENDIF

   6     READ B

   7  ENDWHILE

   8  PRINT A
   ```
   A programmer made a trace table. Here are the first few rows of the table. If the next two inputs are 122 and "N", complete the table and say what the final output of the algorithm is.

Line	A	B	C
1	0		
2	0	Y	
4	0	Y	50
5	50	Y	50
6	50	Y	50

3. Explain in your own words what the algorithm shown in question **2** does.

4. Create an algorithm where the user enters the upper and lower digits of a fraction and the algorithm outputs the fraction as a decimal number.

5. What run-time error might occur with the algorithm you made for question **4**? How would you fix this problem?

6. Write an improved algorithm with less risk of run-time error.

9.4 Development methods

Top-down programming

Instead of making a software application as one big system, programmers break it down into sub-systems. Each sub-system is made separately, then all the sub-systems are fitted together. This makes programming easier and helps with teamwork.

You need to know:
- what top-down programming is
- how to analyse a system into sub-systems.

Fact check

System and sub-systems: Real-life software applications do many different tasks. The complete software application is called a system. The sections that solve different problems are called sub-systems.

Top-down programming: This is a way of making software to meet client needs. This is the process:

1. Analyse the client's overall requirement into smaller tasks or problems to be solved.
2. Write a program to solve each problem.
3. Fit the programs together to make a large program made of many parts.

Teamwork: Most programmers nowadays work in teams. The team will work together to make the complete application. Each person in the team may create a different sub-system. Top-down programming helps with dividing up the work.

Top-down programming has many advantages:

- It lets programmers plan the task in full before they begin programming.
- It breaks a big difficult task down into smaller and easier tasks.
- The different tasks can be given to different people, so the work is done more quickly.
- Each sub-system can be tested to make sure it works perfectly before all the sub-systems are fitted together.

You have learned that every program or algorithm turns inputs into outputs. When you break a program down into sub-systems you must define the inputs and outputs of that sub-system. When you fit the sub-systems together, the complete application should work and meet the client's overall requirement.

Check your readiness

A software application lets people send short text messages to their friends. What sub-systems would this application include?

Structure diagrams

A structure diagram shows how a system is broken down into sub-systems. Each sub-system is shown as a box. They are shown in an upside-down tree structure. Sometimes sub-systems are broken down into even smaller parts.

Fact check

A software application is made of smaller sub-systems. A structure diagram is a drawing of the computer system. It shows the sub-systems in visual form.

Programmers draw structure diagrams to:
- plan the work that needs to be done
- share the plan with the team of programmers
- check the work as it is completed.

Every system and sub-system is shown as a box. At the top of the tree is a box with the name of the whole system in it. The sub-systems are shown in the level below.

When drawing a structure diagram, you can add several levels to the chart, which break sub-systems down into even smaller parts. You can continue until the task is split into the simplest possible parts.

To make sure your structure diagram is correct, you must check the following:
- Every function of the software is included in the chart
- Every function appears once only
- The sub-systems are distinct with no overlap
- The sub-systems are the simplest possible parts

Here is an example of a structure chart. It shows sub-systems of a word processing application.

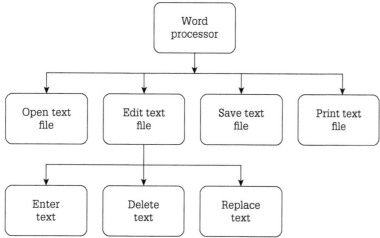

Structure chart for a word processing application

Check your readiness

In the previous topic, you analysed the sub-systems of a messaging application. Draw a structure chart of the application.

Code libraries

> Routines are small sub-programs. A sub-routine does a single task. Sub-routines can be reused in new programs. Programmers sometimes share reusable sub-routines in code libraries.

You need to know:
- what sub-routines, predefined functions and code libraries are
- how to use them in your programs.

Fact check

Sub-systems: Software applications are developed as sub-systems. This is top-down programming.

Other names of sub-systems are:

- sub-program
- routine
- sub-routine.

These names all mean the same thing.

A typical sub-routine will carry out a single task.

Types of sub-routine: There are two types of sub-routine:

- Functions create an output value
- Procedures (also called sub-procedures) carry out tasks but do not supply any output value.

Some functions are so useful that they are part of Python code. These are called predefined functions. You have used many predefined functions in your Python programs. For example:

- `print()`
- `input()`
- `int()`
- `float()`

Programmers also make their own procedures and functions. They might use them in one application. They might reuse these sub-routines in many programming projects in order to save time and reduce errors.

Modules: Programmers sometimes collect together a lot of useful sub-routines that do similar things. They store them in a big file called a module.

Code library: Modules can be stored together as a code library of useful free routines. You get a free code library of useful modules when you download Python.

You can use any of these stored modules in your program. At the top of your program type the word "import" and the name of the module you want to use. Then you can use any of the procedures and functions from that module in your program.

Check your readiness

Research the following features of Python:

- its predefined functions
- its modules and what sub-routines they contain.

9.4 Knowledge test

1. What is top-down programming?

2. What are the advantages of top-down programming?

3. A software application lets you use your phone as an alarm clock to wake you up at the right time in the morning. What sub-systems might be included in this application?

4. Draw a structure diagrams to show the sub-systems you have listed in question **3**. Break at least one sub-system down into even smaller parts.

5. What are the features of a well-designed structure chart?

6. What are predefined functions?

7. What is a module?

8. What is a code library?

9. Why is it useful for a programmer to reuse sub-routines from a previous program?

Exam preparation

1. Use the information contained in topic 9.1 to describe the meaning of the following terms:
   a Verification
   b Validation

Exam-style questions

1. You have written a program that expects you to enter 5 whole numbers between 0 and 100.
   a list **three** sets of test data to test the operation of your program
   b for each set of test data in part **a**, describe:
   i the reason you chose it (each reason must be different)
   ii what you expect to happen.
2. a Complete the trace table for the following pseudocode routine using the test data:
   10, 2, 25, 3, 1, 16, 5, 8, 12, 8, 10

```
Count ← 0

Total ← 0

INPUT Max

FOR LoopCount ← 1 TO Max

 INPUT Number

 Total ← Total + Number

 Count ← Count + 1

NEXT LoopCount

OUTPUT Total / Count
```

Count	Total	Max	LoopCount	Number	OUTPUT

   b Describe the purpose of the algorithm.

10 Databases

This page summarises what you will learn about hardware. Tick the boxes on this page when you are confident you have learned each item.

10.1 Database design

TICK WHEN YOU HAVE LEARNED:

☐ the meaning of key terms such as "data table", "record", "field" and "entity"

☐ how to design a data table to store given data

☐ how to select suitable data types

☐ how to define a primary key and select a suitable primary key

☐ how to explain what makes a good database design.

10.2 Database queries

TICK WHEN YOU HAVE LEARNED:

☐ what a query is, and what a query-by-example is

☐ how to write a query-by-example that selects some fields for display

☐ how to produce a sorted output from a query-by-example

☐ how to write a query-by-example that selects some records for display.

10.1 Database design

Records and fields

Data can be stored in a grid called a table. Each row of the table stores all the facts about a single entity. This store of facts is called a record. Every column of the table stores one fact. This is called a field.

You need to know:
- what a database table is
- what records and fields are
- how to make a database table to match a requirement.

Fact check

Storing data: A database is a way for computers to store data in an organised way. A common method is to store data in a table structure.

Table: Every database is made of one or more tables. A table is a grid of data.

Entities: Data means facts. The facts must be about something. They might be facts about people, objects, events etc. These things are called the entities.

Record: One row of the data table is called a record. A record holds all the data about a single entity. A typical real-life computer database may have thousands or even millions of records.

Fields: One column of the data table is called a field. Each field stores one fact. The table stores the same facts about each entity in the table.

Here is an example of a database. It stores data about chemical elements.

Atomic number	Atomic weight	Name	Symbol	Melting point (°C)	Boiling point (°C)	When discovered
1	1.0079	Hydrogen	H	-259	-253	1776
2	4.0026	Helium	He	-272	-269	1895
7	14.0067	Nitrogen	N	-210	-196	1772
8	15.9994	Oxygen	O	-218	-183	1774
17	35.453	Chlorine	Cl	-101	-35	1774
27	58.9332	Cobalt	Co	1495	2870	1735
28	58.6934	Nickel	Ni	1453	2732	1751
78	195.078	Platinum	Pt	1772	3827	1735

Check your readiness

What are the entities in this table? How many records are there in this table? How many fields are there in this table? Do some research and add three more records to the table.

Data types

The computer uses different methods to store different data types. When you make a database you may have to choose a name and a data type for every field in the database. Text fields cannot be used in calculations.

You need to know:
- what data types are
- what data types to use when designing a database.

Fact check

Data storage: A computer uses different methods to store different types of data. When you store data in a computer you must choose a data type. The data type tells the computer what storage method to use. When you make a data table you must choose what fields to include. Each field stores one fact. For each field, you should choose:

- the field name
- the data type.

Main data types:

- Character – this can store any character you can type in at the keyboard.
- Text – this can store a series of characters making a word, a sentence, or even a book.
- Boolean – this can store True/False values.
- Number – this can store numerical values that represent quantities.
- Date and time – these are special formats that let you store date and time values in suitable structures.

You must think about what type of data you want to store when you pick a data type. Typically, character fields cannot be used in calculations. Number fields cannot hold anything except digits, the minus sign and the decimal point.

Code numbers are made of digits but you should store them in text fields. This is because you cannot use code numbers in calculations. For example, phone numbers are not used in calculations.

Check your readiness

In the previous topic you looked at the table of chemical elements. Choose the right data types for the different fields in the table you produced. Think of three more fields you could add to the table. What data types are they?

Primary key

One field in every table is called the primary key. This stores data that is unique to each record. The primary key is used to identify each record so that records don't get mixed up.

You need to know:
- what a primary key is
- how to pick a suitable primary key for a data table.

Fact check

Data table: Each record in the data table stores facts about one entity. The fields are the facts that you will store about each entity.

In a well-designed data table:

- Each field stores only one fact.
- Each fact is contained in only one field.
- Each fact is stored only once.

Identifying records: One field in the data table must be the primary key. The primary key is a unique field. The data in the primary key field is different for every record in the data table. The primary key can be used to identify each record in the database.

Almost all data tables include a primary key. The primary key is usually a code. The primary key is usually the first field in the table. The code is chosen when the record is first added to the database table. A code can be made of numbers or letters or both. A code field is always the text data type.

Some databases have more than one table. Each table will have a different primary key. The primary key from one table can be stored in another table. This makes a link between tables. A database with links between tables is called a relational database.

Check your readiness

What field would you use as the primary key for the table of chemical elements? There is more than one possible answer.

10.1 Knowledge test

The test questions refer to the following data table:

Code	Island's name	Area (sq miles)	Country	Population
01	Greenland	822 700	Greenland and Denmark	56 000
02	New Guinea	303 381	Indonesia and Papua New Guinea	11 000 000
03	Borneo	288 869	Indonesia, Malaysia, Brunei	19 800 000
04	Madagascar	226 917	Madagascar	25 000 000
05	Baffin Island	195 928	Canada	10 745
06	Sumatra	171 069	Indonesia	50 000 000
07	Honshu	87 200	Japan	103 000 000
08	Victoria Island	83 897	Canada	1875

1. What is an entity? What are the entities in this data table?

2. What is a record? How many records are there in this data table?

3. What is a field? How many fields are there in this data table?

4. What are the names of the fields? What data type would you use for each field?

5. What is a primary key? What field would you use as a primary key? Explain your reasons.

10.2 Database queries

Select fields

> A query lets you choose part of the data in a database. A query-by-example is a way of telling the computer what fields and records to display. It also lets you sort the data.

You need to know:
- what a query-by-example is
- how to select fields from a database using a query-by-example.

Fact check

Query: This is a computer command that picks out records and fields from a database. You can use data queries to pick out the data that you want from a large database.

Query-by-example: This is a method of making a query. You specify:

- what fields you want to see
- what records you want to see.

The computer will display data that matches your query.

When making a query-by-example you first make a table that shows every field in the database. In the example below, every field comes from the table of elements you have already worked with.

	Atomic number	Atomic weight	Name	Symbol	Melting point (°C)	Boiling point (°C)	When discovered
Table	Elements	Elements	Elements	Elements	Elements	Elements	Elements
Show	✔		✔	✔			✔
Sort							Ascending

You enter YES (or a tick) under each field that you want to see.

You can also sort the table – either ordered as ascending (going up) or descending (going down).

Check your readiness

A computer user entered the query-by-example shown on this page. Create a table that shows the data that the computer would display.

Select records

> A query-by-example can include search criteria. By including criteria you can select some records for display. The criteria can specify an exact match. Alternatively, you can use relational operators and logical operators to create a more complex query.

You need to know:
- how to select fields from a database using a query-by-example.

Fact check

Query-by-example using search criteria: A query can select one or more records from a data table. Only the selected records will be shown.

The simplest way to select records is using a match. You enter text into the query table. This is called the search criteria. The computer will find all records that match the search criteria.

Here is a query-by-example that includes search criteria.

	Atomic number	Atomic weight	Name	Symbol	Melting point (°C)	Boiling point (°C)	When discovered
Table	Elements	Elements	Elements	Elements	Elements	Elements	Elements
Show			✔				
Sort							
Criteria							= 1774

This query would show the name of all elements discovered in the year 1774. If you look back to the table on page 148, you will see that these are:

- Oxygen
- Chlorine.

You can combine more than one criteria. To do this you add more rows to the data table. Each new row starts with a logical connector such as AND, OR and NOT. You have already learned what these connectors mean.

	Atomic number	Atomic weight	Name	Symbol	Melting point (°C)	Boiling point (°C)	When discovered
Table	Elements	Elements	Elements	Elements	Elements	Elements	Elements
Show	✔		✔	✔			
Sort	Ascending						
Criteria							= 1774
OR							= 1776

The query above will show the atomic number, name and symbol of all elements discovered in the year 1774 or 1776. The list is sorted by atomic number in ascending order.

Atomic number	Name	Symbol
1	Hydrogen	H
8	Oxygen	O
17	Chlorine	Cl

As well as looking for matches you can use relational operators such as > and <. The computer will find records that match the comparison.

	Atomic number	Atomic weight	Name	Symbol	Melting point (°C)	Boiling point (°C)	When discovered
Table	Elements	Elements	Elements	Elements	Elements	Elements	Elements
Show	✔	✔		✔	✔		
Sort					Ascending		
Criteria					> 0		

This query selects atomic number, atomic weight, symbol and melting point. It selects elements with a melting point greater than 0°. The display is sorted by melting point in ascending order.

Here is the result of this query.

Atomic number	Atomic weight	Symbol	Melting point (°C)
28	58.6934	Ni	1453
27	58.9332	Co	1495
78	195.078	Pt	1772

Check your readiness

Work with another student. Create a query-by-example for the table of elements. Swap queries. Make a table to match the query you were given.

10.2 Knowledge test

These test questions refer to the following data table:

Code	Island's name	Area (sq miles)	Country	Population
01	Greenland	822 700	Greenland and Denmark	56 000
02	New Guinea	303 381	Indonesia and Papua New Guinea	11 000 000
03	Borneo	288 869	Indonesia, Malaysia, Brunei	19 800 000
04	Madagascar	226 917	Madagascar	25 000 000
05	Baffin Island	195 928	Canada	10 745
06	Sumatra	171 069	Indonesia	50 000 000
07	Honshu	87 200	Japan	103 000 000
08	Victoria Island	83 897	Canada	1875

1. Create a query-by-example to view islands within Canada. The query will display only the name and population of each island. Sort in order of area, starting with the smaller island.

2. Show the output you would see from the query-by-example in question **1**.

3. Create a query-by-example to display the name, area and population of all islands with more than 1000 000 inhabitants. Sort alphabetically by name.

4. Show the output you would see from the query-by-example in question **3**.

5. Create a query-by-example that would show all details of islands with an area greater than 100 000 square miles and a population less than 100 000 people.

6. Show the output you would see from the query-by-example in question **5**.

Exam preparation

1. Use the information contained in topic 10.1 to describe the meaning of the following terms:
   a Field
   b Record
   c Primary Key.

Exam-style questions

This is the database from section 10.1 and it is called PERIODIC TABLE. The questions will relate to this database.

Atomic number	Atomic weight	Name	Symbol	Melting point (°C)	Boiling point (°C)	When discovered
1	1.0079	Hydrogen	H	-259	-253	1776
2	4.0026	Helium	He	-272	-269	1895
7	14.0067	Nitrogen	N	-210	-196	1772
8	15.9994	Oxygen	O	-218	-183	1774
17	35.453	Chlorine	Cl	-101	-35	1774
27	58.9332	Cobalt	Co	1495	2870	1735
28	58.6934	Nickel	Ni	1453	2732	1751
78	195.078	Platinum	Pt	1772	3827	1735

1. State which field in this database you would recommend as the primary key and why you chose it.
2. State the data type you would use for each of the following fields:

Field	Data Type
Atomic Weight	
Name	
Symbol	
Melting Point (°C)	

3. The query-by-example grid below is to be used to provide a list of all the elements with a boiling point above 0 °C. The output is to include the name of the element, its symbol, its atomic number, its atomic weight and the boiling point, and should be sorted alphabetically by name. Complete this query-by-example table for the given search criteria.

Field:					
Table:					
Sort:					
Show:	❏	❏	❏	❏	❏
Criteria:					
or:					

Appendices

Appendix A: Binary and hexadecimal

This table shows the binary numbers from 0 0 0 0 to 1 1 1 1 with their hexadecimal and denary equivalents.

Binary	Hexadecimal	Denary
0000 0000	0	0
0000 0001	1	1
0000 0010	2	2
0000 0011	3	3
0000 0100	4	4
0000 0101	5	5
0000 0110	6	6
0000 0111	7	7
0000 1000	8	8
0000 1001	9	9
0000 1010	A	10
0000 1011	B	11
0000 1100	C	12
0000 1101	D	13
0000 1110	E	14
0000 1111	F	15

The binary grid

Insert an eight-bit binary number into this grid. Add up the value of all columns with a 1 in them to get the denary value.

128	64	32	16	8	4	2	1

The extended binary grid

Use this grid for converting numbers larger than 1 byte into denary.

32768	16384	8192	4096	2048	1024	512	256	128	64	32	16	8	4	2	1

The hexadecimal grid

Enter a two-digit hexadecimal number into the grid. Multiply digit value by column value. Add the results together. This will give you the denary value.

16	1

The extended hexadecimal grid

Enter any hexadecimal number of up to four digits into the grid. Multiply digit value by column value. Add the results together. This will give the denary value.

4096	256	16	1

Appendix B: Logic gates

NOT

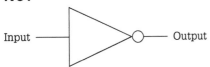

A	NOT A
0	1
1	0

AND

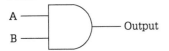

A	B	A AND B
0	0	0
0	1	0
1	0	0
1	1	1

OR

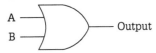

A	B	A AND B
0	0	0
0	1	1
1	0	1
1	1	1

XOR

A	B	A AND B
0	0	0
0	1	1
1	0	1
1	1	0

NAND

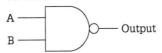

A	B	A AND B
0	0	1
0	1	1
1	0	1
1	1	0

NOR

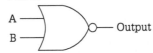

A	B	A AND B
0	0	1
0	1	0
1	0	0
1	1	0

Appendix C: Python commands and structures

Feature	Remember	Example
Comments	Comments begin with # The computer ignores comments.	`#This is a comment`
Variable = value	A value is stored in a variable.	`Age = 21` `Password = "Sesame"`
Data types	Integer = a whole number Floating point = a number with a decimal String = text characters Strings are enclosed in quotation marks (single or double).	

`print ()`	The word "print" is in lower case
	
	followed by brackets.
	
	Inside the brackets – a string, a value or a variable.
		`print ("This is a print command")`
		`print (1+2)`
		`print (Age)`

`input ()`	The word "input" is in lower case followed by brackets. Inside the brackets – the prompt. This is often used with a variable. Input variables are always string data type.	`Variable = input ("Prompt")`
Data type conversion	`int ()` converts a variable to integer data type `float ()` converts a variable to floating point data type.	`Age = int (Age)` `Cost = float (Cost)`

Arithmetic operators	These can be used with numbers or with variables that store numbers:
	
	  + addition
	  - subtraction
	  * multiply
	  / divide.
		`Variable = 16 / 4`
		`Variable = Variable + 1`

Relational operators	These are used to compare two values in a logical test. The result of the comparison can be True or False.
	
	The relational operators are:
	
	  == equal
	  != not equal
	  < smaller than
	  > bigger than
		`12 > 6`
		
		`99 == 120/ 2`

Feature	Remember	Example
if	The word if appears, then a logical test, then a colon. The lines that follow the colon are indented. The indented commands are carried out if the result of the test is True.	```if Age > 18:``` ``` print("Too old")```

else	This always comes after an if statement.
	The word else is followed by a colon.
	The lines that follow the colon are indented.
	The indented commands are carried out if the result of the test is True.
		```if Age > 18:```
		``` print("Too old")```
		```else:```
		``` print("Just right")```

for loop	This uses a counter variable, usually the letter i For i in range (min, max) : min and max are numbers, they are the start and stop values. The lines that follow the colon are indented. The indented commands are repeated in the loop. The loop counts from the start value to 1 less than the stop value.	```for i in range (1, 12):``` ``` print(i * 10)```

while loop	This uses a logical test.
	while test:
	The lines that follow the colon are indented.
	The indented commands are repeated while the result of the test is True.
	Before the loop: set the value used in the test.
	Inside the test: change the value used in the test.
		```Password = "xxx"```
		```while Password != "Sesame":```
		``` Password = input("Enter```
		``` password")```
		```print("Correct")```

Make a list	Lists are data structures made of elements.
	You can make an empty list.
	You can make a list with several elements already in place.
		```Studentlist = []```
		```Studentlist =["Jim", "Abdullah",```
		```"Lakshmi"]```

Append to a list	Append means add a value to a list. The value will be added as an extra element at the end of the list.	```Studentlist.append("Shirley")```
Print a list	If you print the whole list it will be printed in square brackets.	```print(Studentlist)```

Print the elements of a list	You can use a for loop to print the elements of a list one at a time.
	This is a better way to print a list.
		```Listlength = len(Studentlist)```
		```For i in range(Listlength) :```
		``` print(Studentlist[i])```

Appendix D: Writing pseudocode

Feature	Remember	Example
`PRINT`	The word `PRINT` is followed by a string, a value or a variable .	`PRINT "Welcome to the game"`
`READ`	The word `READ` is followed by the name of a variable. Data is input to the variable.	`READ Password`
`Variable ← value`	The arrow symbol assigns a value to a variable.	`Password ← "Sesame"`
Arithmetic operators	These can be used with numbers or with variables that store numbers: + addition - subtraction * multiply / divide	`Count = Count + 1`
Relational operators	These are used to compare two values in a logical test. The result of the comparison can be True or False. The relational operators are: = equal <> not equal < smaller than > bigger than	`Password <> "Sesame"`

`IF`	The word `IF` is followed by a logical test and the word `THEN`
	The commands that follow `THEN` will be carried out if the result of the test is True.
	The structure ends with the word `ENDIF`
	Unlike in Python the whole IF structure can be shown on one line
	
	`IF test THEN... ENDIF`
	or it can be on several lines.
		`READ Password`
		`IF Password <> "Sesame" THEN`
		`    PRINT("Incorrect")`
		`ENDIF`

Feature	Remember	Example

`ELSE`	The word `ELSE` comes within an `IF` statement. The commands that follow `ELSE` will be carried out if the result of the test is False.	```READ Password
		IF Password <> "Sesame" THEN
		    PRINT ("Incorrect")
		ELSE
		    PRINT ("Correct")
		ENDIF```

`While` loop	The word `WHILE` comes first, then a logical test, then the word `DO`. The commands that follow `DO` are repeated if the result of the test is True. The structure ends with the word `ENDWHILE`	```READ Password
		WHILE Password <> "Sesame" DO
		    READ Password
		ENDWHILE```

`REPEAT... UNTIL` loop	The word `REPEAT` comes first. The commands that follow are repeated. Then the word `UNTIL` appears and a test. When the result of the test is True the loop stops.	```REPEAT READ Password UNTIL Password = "Sesame"```

`FOR... NEXT` loop	This is a counter-controlled loop. It has this general structure:
	`FOR i ← Min TO Max`
	`....`
	`NEXT i`
	Instead of min and max, type the minimum and maximum values. The loop will count from the minimum to the maximum value.
		``FOR i ← 1 TO 12
		    PRINT i * 10
		NEXT i```

Declare an array	An array is similar to a list. To create an empty array you declare it. This means you specify the number of elements in the array.	`StudentName [1:30]`

Put values into an array		```FOR i ← 1 TO 30
		    INPUT Name
		    StudentName [i] ← Name
		Next i```

Print elements of an array		```FOR i ← 1 TO 30 PRINT StudentName [i] Next i```

Appendix E: Drawing flowcharts

Start and end boxes

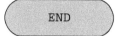

Input and output boxes

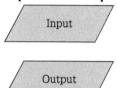

Assign value box

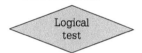

Decision box

if structure

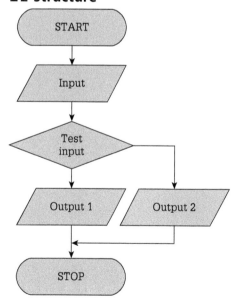

Loop structure

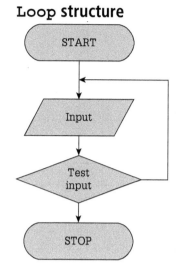

Appendix F: Query-by-example

The table for a query-by-example should have a column for every field in the database.

It has the following rows.

	Field 1	Field 2	Field 3	etc. . .
Table				
Show				
Sort				
Criteria				

To specify a query-by-example:

- In the first row (Table): Put the name of the table that the field appears in.
- In the second row (Show): Put a tick under each field you want to display.
- In the third row (Sort): Put the words "Ascending" or "Descending" under **one** field to specify a sort order. This row may be left blank. The records will be shown in an unsorted order.
- In the fourth row (Criteria): Specify the records you want to see by entering search criteria. If you leave this row blank, all records will be shown.

To specify search criteria:

- Give an exact match to the value you want to see using = (the equals sign).
- Say the range you want to see using a relational operator such as >

You can add extra search criteria. The new rows should begin with a logical operator such as AND, OR or NOT to explain how the different criteria will be combined.

Answers to knowledge test questions

1 Data representation

1.1 Binary systems

Question number	Answer	Is your answer correct? (Tick)	If you did not give the correct answer, reread this section
1	Computers transform data into information. Information is data that has been organised. Information is more meaningful and useful than data.		*1.1 Binary data*
2	"Binary" means anything that can be in two states. The two states are often represented by 1 and 0.		*1.1 Binary data*
3	Binary is base 2. There are two digits. Each position value in the number is worth two more than the previous digit. Denary is base 10. There are ten digits. Each digit is worth ten more than the previous digit.		*1.1 Binary and denary*
4	Computer Science students learn about binary numbers because all data inside the computer is represented using on/off electrical signals. Binary numbers are used to represent the two states.		*1.1 Binary data*
5	A bit in RAM is represented as a switch that either transmits an electrical signal or not.		*1.1 Bits and bytes*
6	Inside the computer, bits are organised into groups of eight called bytes.		*1.1 Bits and bytes*
7	The capacity of RAM is measured in kilobytes, megabytes and gigabytes.		*1.1 Bits and bytes*
8	The processor can access data in RAM quickly, so the more data that can be held in RAM the faster the computer works.		*1.1 Bits and bytes*
9	0 0 0 1 0 0 0 0 0 0 0 1 0 0 0 1 0 0 0 1 0 0 1 0 0 0 0 1 0 0 1 1 0 0 0 1 0 1 0 0 0 0 0 1 0 1 0 1 0 0 0 1 0 1 1 0		*1.1 Counting in binary*
10	See the binary grid following this table.		*1.1 Convert binary to denary*
11	See the extended binary grid following this table.		*1.1 Convert binary to denary*

Question number	Answer	Is your answer correct? (Tick)	If you did not give the correct answer, reread this section
12	0 1 1 0 0 0 1 1 = 99 0 0 1 1 1 1 0 0 = 60 1 0 1 1 1 1 0 1 = 189 1 1 0 0 1 1 0 1 = 205 1 0 1 0 1 0 1 0 0 = 340		*1.1 Convert binary to denary*
13	81 = 0 1 0 1 0 0 0 1 106 = 0 1 1 0 1 0 1 0 217 = 1 1 0 1 1 0 0 1 290 = 1 0 0 1 0 0 0 1 0 1010 = 1 1 1 1 1 1 0 0 1 0		*1.1 Convert denary to binary*

Question 10 answer:

128	64	32	16	8	4	2	1

Question 11 answer:

32 768	16 384	8192	4096	2048	1024	512	256	128	64	32	16	8	4	2	1

1.2 Hexadecimal

Question number	Answer	Is your answer correct? (Tick)	If you did not give the correct answer, reread this section
1	It is easier to read and write hexadecimal numbers than binary numbers.		*1.2 How hexadecimal is used*
2	It is easier to convert hexadecimal numbers to binary.		*1.2 Hexadecimal and binary*
3	Hexadecimal numbers are used to represent memory addresses, machine code instructions and colour codes.		*1.2 How hexadecimal is used*
4	3F = 63 90 = 144 AD = 173 D6 = 214		*1.2 What is hexadecimal?*
5	73 = 49 166 = A6 91 = 5B 204 = CC		*1.2 Hexadecimal and denary*

Question number	Answer	Is your answer correct? (Tick)	If you did not give the correct answer, reread this section
6	123 = 291 A1A = 2586		*1.2 Hexadecimal and denary*
7	270 = 10E 3072 = C00		*1.2 Hexadecimal and denary*
8	0 0 0 1 0 0 0 1 1 1 1 0 = 11E 1 1 1 1 0 0 0 0 1 1 1 1 = FOF 1 1 0 1 1 0 1 0 0 1 1 1 = DA7		*1.2 Hexadecimal and binary*
9	BB3 = 1 0 1 1 1 0 1 1 0 0 1 1 ABC = 1 0 1 0 1 0 1 1 1 1 00 99E = 1 0 0 1 1 0 0 1 1 1 1 0		*1.2 Hexadecimal and binary*

1.3 Data storage

Question number	Answer	Is your answer correct? (Tick)	If you did not give the correct answer, reread this section
1	The largest binary number you can make with eight bits (one byte) is 255.		*1.3 Digital data*
2	Floating point numbers store fractions. The computer stores the digits of the number using one or more bytes. It stores the position of the point in another byte.		*1.3 Digital data*
3	The computer stores text characters by using a number code such as ASCII or Unicode.		*1.3 Digital data*
4	A bitmap image stores each pixel as a separate number representing the colour of that point		*1.3 Digital graphics*
5	Bitmap graphics produce realistic detailed images but they are very large. When increased in size they lose image quality.		*1.3 Digital graphics*
6	A vector graphic file stores an image as a collection of shapes constructed from lines. It stores formulas that allow the computer to draw the image.		*1.3 Digital graphics*
7	Vector graphics use less storage space than bitmaps and produce clear images that can be scaled up or down in size with no loss of quality. Vector graphics are not suitable for photographs and other realistic colour images.		*1.3 Digital graphics*

Question number	Answer	Is your answer correct? (Tick)	If you did not give the correct answer, reread this section
8	WAV: Sound content stored to a high-quality standard and large file size. MP3: Sound content stored at a reduced file size, with lower-quality standards. MIDI: Sound content stored as a series of instructions that can be interpreted by a synthesiser. MP4: Video content.		*1.3 Digital sound and video*
9	The quality of an audio file is determined by sample rate per second, number of channels and bit depth (the range of sound frequencies used).		*1.3 Digital sound and video*
10	Lossless compression is reduction in file size without loss of quality. Lossy compression is reduction in file size associated with loss of data quality.		*1.3 Compression*
11	Images can be reduced in size by storing blocks of identical colour using a single colour code. Another method is to reduce the colour depth (the range of colours used).		*1.3 Compression*

2 Communications and the Internet

2.1 Data transmission

Question number	Answer	Is your answer correct? (Tick)	If you did not give the correct answer, reread this section
1	The three main types of cable are twisted pair, coaxial and fibre-optic cable.		*2.1 How data is transmitted*
2	Twisted pair cable is cheap and flexible, but prone to interference. Coaxial cable is resistant to electrical interference, but it is inflexible and expensive. Fibre-optic cable is reliable and secure, but somewhat expensive.		*2.1 How data is transmitted*
3	Wireless transmission is an alternative to using cable.		*2.1 How data is transmitted*
4	In serial transmission the eight bits of a byte are sent one after the other along the same medium. In parallel transmission the eight bits are sent at the same time along eight different transmission media.		*2.1 Serial or parallel?*

Question number	Answer	Is your answer correct? (Tick)	If you did not give the correct answer, reread this section
5	Serial transmission is somewhat slower than parallel transmission but it is reliable over distance. For that reason it is used to connect computers with peripherals and with other computers.		*2.1 Serial or parallel?*
6	Parallel transmission is faster than serial transmission but less reliable over distance. For this reason it is used where speed is most important and distances are short – within the processor.		*2.1 Serial or parallel?*
7	USB means universal serial bus. It is a standard for connectivity. It is used to connect peripherals to the processor.		*2.1 Data bus*
8	The transmitter sends a signal. The receiver checks for errors. If there are no errors, it sends an acknowledgement. If no acknowledgement is received, the transmitter sends the signal again.		*2.1 Transmission errors*
9	1 0 1 1 1 0 0 1 × ERROR 0 0 1 1 1 0 0 1 ✔ 1 1 1 1 0 0 0 0 ✔		*2.1 Parity check*
10	8409981 – 9 ✔ 7845232 – 1 ✔ 6654914 – 0 × ERROR (should be 5)		*2.1 Check digit and checksum*
11	A simple check digit will not detect transposition errors, as the total of the digits will not be affected.		*2.1 Check digit and checksum*
12	22910127		*2.1 Check digit and checksum*

2.2 The Internet

Question number	Answer	Is your answer correct? (Tick)	If you did not give the correct answer, reread this section
1	Connecting to the Internet requires a data transmission medium, Internet software and shared protocols.		*2.2 What is the Internet?*
2	An ISP is an Internet service provider. It is a company that helps you connect to the Internet, sending signals between the Internet and your computer. It may also provide email and web hosting.		*2.2 What is the Internet?*

Question number	Answer	Is your answer correct? (Tick)	If you did not give the correct answer, reread this section
3	Web page: This is a multimedia document that can be copied to your computer over an Internet connection. Website: This is a collection of linked web pages. Web server : This is a computer with a permanent Internet link that holds one or more websites.		*2.2 What is the World Wide Web?*
4	A web browser receives a copy of a web page over an Internet connection and displays the web page on your computer. It may also take your response and send it back.		*2.2 What is the World Wide Web?*
5	Hypertext is text that makes a link to a web page. When you click on the hyperlink the linked page will open.		*2.2 HTML*
6	Markup is a way of adding computer code to a document to change the way it is displayed or to add active commands.		*2.2 HTML*
7	HTML tags typically come in pairs because one tag turns a feature on, and the second tag turns it off (e.g. bold text).		*2.2 HTML*
8	HTTP is the protocol that controls connectivity to web pages through their unique addresses.		*2.2 HTTP: Hypertext transfer protocol*
9	HTTPS is like HTTP but it has extra features that improve security – encryption and authentication.		*2.2 HTTP: Hypertext transfer protocol*
10	TCP means "transmission control protocol". It controls the way that data carried over the Internet is divided into packets. IP means "Internet protocol". It makes sure that data packets are sent to the right address.		*2.2 TCP/IP*
11	An IP address identifies a website with a number and a URL identifies a website with meaningful text.		*2.2 TCP/IP*
12	In the website address http://global.oup.com/about the top-level domain is **.com** the domain name is **global.oup.com** the path is **/about**		*2.2 TCP/IP*

2.3 Safety online

Question number	Answer	Is your answer correct? (Tick)	If you did not give the correct answer, reread this section
1	Don't meet them. Tell an adult you trust.		*2.3 Staying safe*
2	You should not give your Internet passwords to anyone.		*2.3 Staying safe*
3	Virus: This hides inside other files. Trojan: This disguises itself as a useful or an interesting file. Worm: This is held in a file that does not show up when you list files on your computer.		*2.3 Malware and hacking*
4	To avoid getting malware on a computer: Do not download free content from websites. Do not open files attached to emails. Only use storage devices sold by reliable retailers.		*2.3 Malware and hacking*
5	Anti-virus software: • identifies malware in files on your computer • removes malware from your computer • checks data coming into your computer • warns you about online risks.		*2.3 Protective software*
6	A firewall can be hardware or software or both. A firewall checks all data passing in or out of a network to remove malware and other risks.		*2.3 Protective software*

3 The processor

3.1 Logic gates

The six logic gates are listed in Appendix B of this Revision Guide. Check your answers against this list. If you have made any mistakes, refer back to the relevant section.

3.2 Logical processing

Question number	Answer	Is your answer correct? (Tick)	If you did not give the correct answer, reread this section
1	A AND (NOT B)		*3.2 Simplify statements*
2			*3.2 Logic circuits*

Question number	Answer					Is your answer correct? (Tick)	If you did not give the correct answer, reread this section
3	<table><tr><td>A</td><td>B</td><td>C (NOT B)</td><td>D (A AND C)</td></tr><tr><td>0</td><td>0</td><td>1</td><td>0</td></tr><tr><td>0</td><td>1</td><td>0</td><td>0</td></tr><tr><td>1</td><td>0</td><td>1</td><td>1</td></tr><tr><td>1</td><td>1</td><td>0</td><td>0</td></tr></table>						*3.2 Truth tables and circuits*
4	The output is True when A is True and B is False.						*3.2 Solve a problem*
5	(A NOR B) OR (B AND C)						*3.2 Repeat inputs*
6	<table><tr><td>A</td><td>B</td><td>C</td><td>D (A NOR B)</td><td>E (B AND C)</td><td>F (D OR E)</td></tr><tr><td>0</td><td>0</td><td>0</td><td>1</td><td>0</td><td>1</td></tr><tr><td>0</td><td>0</td><td>1</td><td>1</td><td>0</td><td>1</td></tr><tr><td>0</td><td>1</td><td>0</td><td>0</td><td>0</td><td>0</td></tr><tr><td>0</td><td>1</td><td>1</td><td>0</td><td>1</td><td>1</td></tr><tr><td>1</td><td>0</td><td>0</td><td>0</td><td>0</td><td>0</td></tr><tr><td>1</td><td>0</td><td>1</td><td>0</td><td>0</td><td>0</td></tr><tr><td>1</td><td>1</td><td>0</td><td>0</td><td>0</td><td>0</td></tr><tr><td>1</td><td>1</td><td>1</td><td>0</td><td>1</td><td>1</td></tr></table>						*3.2 Repeat inputs*
7	If all inputs are False the output is True.						*3.2 Repeat inputs*

3.3 Inside the CPU

Question number	Answer	Is your answer correct? (Tick)	If you did not give the correct answer, reread this section
1	The main memory stores data and instructions in binary form. The CPU is where data is processed (changed).		*3.3 The central processing unit (CPU)*
2	Each memory location has its own address. The address is a binary number.		*3.3 The central processing unit (CPU)*
3	The two parts of the CPU are the ALU and the control unit.		*3.3 The central processing unit (CPU)*
4	Logic circuits are inside the ALU. The logic circuits change the electrical signals using the rules of arithmetic and logic.		*3.3 The central processing unit (CPU)*
5	The control unit has a timer to make sure all the actions are carried out in order, one after the other.		*3.3 The central processing unit (CPU)*
6	The code that turns instructions into binary numbers is called machine code.		*3.3 The fetch-execute cycle*

Question number	Answer	Is your answer correct? (Tick)	If you did not give the correct answer, reread this section
7	Every CPU has a set of instructions that it knows. Every instruction has a code number. This is called the CPU's instruction set.		*3.3 The fetch-execute cycle*
8	Fetch – the control unit fetches a machine code instruction from main memory. Decode – the control unit decodes the instruction so it knows what action to carry out. Execute – the control unit sends the instruction to the ALU. The ALU carries out the action.		*3.3 The fetch-execute cycle*
9	Instructions and data are stored as electronic numbers in the main memory. The CPU fetches the instructions and data from main memory. The CPU send the results back to main memory.		*3.3 The fetch-execute cycle*
10	**a** The program counter (PC) holds the address of the next instruction to fetch. **b** The memory address register (MAR) holds an address to read from or write to. **c** The instruction register (IR) holds the instruction currently being executed. **d** The memory data register (MDR) holds data just read from memory, or about to be written to memory.		*3.3 Registers and buses*

4 Hardware

4.1 Input devices

Question number	Answer	Is your answer correct? (Tick)	If you did not give the correct answer, reread this section
1	The two devices are the keyboard (used to input text data) and the mouse (used to input positional data).		*4.1 Keyboard and mouse*
2	Disadvantages of manual input devices are as follows: • They are slower than automatic systems. • Human users can make mistakes. • People get tired when typing for a long time.		*4.1 Keyboard and mouse*

Question number	Answer	Is your answer correct? (Tick)	If you did not give the correct answer, reread this section
3	The three types of touch screen are resistive, capacitive and infra-red.		*4.1 Touch screens*
4	Resistive: • The advantages are that this is the least expensive type of screen; also, you can touch the screen with any object and it will detect it. • The disadvantage is that this type of screen is easily damaged. Capacitive: • The advantages are that a capacitive screen is stronger than a resistive screen and it makes a brighter image. • The disadvantage is that you must use your bare finger, not a pen or glove. Infra-red: • The advantages are that this screen gives a strong bright image; also, you can touch the screen with any object. • The disadvantage is that it is more expensive than other types of touch screen.		*4.1 Touch screens*
5	The aperture is the small hole where the light enters the device. The aperture contains a lens. The lens focuses the light onto a sensitive electronic surface.		*4.1 Camera and microphone*
6	The component vibrates when it is hit by sound waves. It turns the vibrations into electrical signals.		*4.1 Camera and microphone*
7	Scanning a barcode is quicker and more accurate than manual data entry. A barcode can be printed by any black and white printer.		*4.1 Barcode readers*
8	A QR code is 2D (two dimensional). It is more complex in design than a barcode and can hold more data.		*4.1 Barcode readers*
9	OMR (optical mark recognition): An OMR scanner reads marks made on paper or card (e.g. to select from a list of choices). OCR (optical character recognition): An OCR scanner takes an image of a document. The scanner can detect the different letters in the document. 3D scanner: A 3D scanner records the whole shape of a solid object. All the information about the object's shape is sent to the computer.		*4.1 Scanners*

Question number	Answer	Is your answer correct? (Tick)	If you did not give the correct answer, reread this section
10	The correct answer could give any three of the following: • Light sensors tell the computer how dark or bright it is. • Temperature sensors tell the computer how warm or cold it is. • Magnetism is used to detect metal objects, or to find a compass direction. • Humidity is used where the presence of moisture is important (e.g. in agriculture, dry storage). • Acidity is important in science, cooking and industry. • Motion can be detected – for example, computer games consoles can detect when they are moved around in the air.		*4.1 Sensors*
11	The computer monitors the effect of its actions and uses this as input. The computer adjusts its actions to maintain a stable state.		*4.1 Control systems*

4.2 Output devices

Question number	Answer	Is your answer correct? (Tick)	If you did not give the correct answer, reread this section
1	LCD A layer of liquid crystal refracts light that passes through it. The refraction changes with the flow of electricity through the liquid crystal. It requires an external source of light. LED An LED is like a small light bulb. It creates light. LED can be used as the light source for LCD. In an OLED display the image is made of thousands of tiny LEDs.		*4.2 Monitors and display*

Question number	Answer			Is your answer correct? (Tick)	If you did not give the correct answer, reread this section
2		Hard copy	Soft copy		4.2 Monitors and display
	Advantages	This is a permanent record that can be used away from the computer. Some people like reading from paper.	This is immediate output as you work at the computer, always changing to reflect what you do.		
	Disadvantages	It is more expensive, takes up space and is worse for the environment.	There is no permanent record. It disappears when the output changes.		
3	An inkjet printer is used for high-quality colour printing when the volume of printing is quite low. A laser printer is used for black and white or colour printing when you need a lot of printing done quickly.				4.2 Printers
4	A plastic or metal cone is fixed to wire coiled around a magnet. Electrical signals make the magnet attract and repel the metal coil. The coil moves up and down, pulling and pushing the cone. The moving cone pumps sounds out into the air.				4.2 Sound
5	An actuator controls a mechanism that moves objects about. In a control system the actuator is controlled by the computer. The computer controls the actuator, based on feedback from sensors.				4.2 Actuators

Question number	Answer	Is your answer correct? (Tick)	If you did not give the correct answer, reread this section
6	A 2D cutter uses a laser to cut away at the surface of some material from a single position. A 2D cutter is used to cut holes or engrave the surface. A 3D cutter uses lasers to cut away material from all angles. A 3D cutter is used to create a solid object. A 3D printer builds up layers from dots of materials (e.g. plastic) to form the object.		*4.2 Manufacturing objects*
7	Output technologies used with mobile devices include: • a modern, flat, lightweight touch screen • speakers in the phone, plus headphones that can be plugged into the phone • actuators that make the phone vibrate.		*4.2 Output in everyday life*
8	CAD/CAM stands for "computer aided design/computer aided manufacture". Objects are designed on the computer screen. When the design is ready, it is sent to a 3D printer that makes the shape. CAD/CAM is used because on the computer you can form designs quickly, test and improve designs before making them, then work out what materials are needed and what the costs will be.		*4.2 Output in everyday life*

4.3 Memory and storage

Question number	Answer	Is your answer correct? (Tick)	If you did not give the correct answer, reread this section
1	Volatile memory is maintained by electricity. When the electricity is switched off, the content of storage is lost.		*4.3 Primary storage*
2	RAM (random access memory) can store new data but it is volatile. ROM (read only memory) is non-volatile but it cannot store new data.		*4.3 Primary storage*
3	Primary storage is directly linked to the processor. Access speed is very fast. Secondary storage offers slower access but it can retain content when the processor is working on other tasks.		*4.3 Measuring storage*

Question number	Answer	Is your answer correct? (Tick)	If you did not give the correct answer, reread this section
4	1 kilobyte = 1024 bytes. 1 megabyte = 1024 kilobytes. 1024 × 1024 = 1 048 576.		*4.3 Measuring storage*
5	To estimate of the size of the text file: 10 pages with 2000 characters on each page = 20 000 characters. Each character requires one byte of storage. So the file is about 20Kb.		*4.3 File sizes*
6	To estimate the size of a bitmap file you need to know: • the number of pixels in the image • the number of bytes used to store the colour of each pixel.		*4.3 File sizes*
7	The bit rate of a sound file is the number of bytes used to store one second of sound.		*4.3 File sizes*
8	The electrical signals of primary storage are converted into spots of magnetism. These spots retain their magnetic charge after the electricity is taken away.		*4.3 Magnetic storage*
9	CDs, DVDs and Blu-ray disks store data as microscopic pits that are read by laser. The pits on DVDs are smaller than CDs, so more data can be stored on the disk. Blu-ray uses the smallest pits of all.		*4.3 Optical storage*
10	Flash memory is a good choice because it is small, light and robust, with high storage capacity and read/write access. The main limiting factor is the cost, which is higher than magnetic storage.		*4.3 Solid state (flash) storage*
11	Magnetic tape is suitable for backup because it is cheap with high storage capacity. Backup requires a lot of capacity because you should backup all your other storage. Magnetic tape is not suitable for more general use because speed of access is very slow.		*4.3 Use and choice of storage*
12	Cloud storage is remote storage accessed via an Internet connection to a remote server.		*4.3 Use and choice of storage*

5 Software

5.1 Systems software

Question number	Answer	Is your answer correct? (Tick)	If you did not give the correct answer, reread this section
1	Application software does work that is useful to the human user. System software controls the operation of the computer itself.		*5.1 What is software?*
2	Loading software: The instructions are copied into the main memory of the computer (RAM). Running software: The computer executes the instruction in RAM.		*5.1 What is software?*
3	Different types of computer use different operating systems. Software is usually written to run with a particular operating system. The software is compatible with that operating system.		*5.1 Operating systems*
4	Four functions of an operating system are: • controlling hardware • providing a user interface • loading and running software • handling errors and problems.		*5.1 Functions of an operating system*
5	This is what happens during boot up: • The basic BIOS instructions are taken from ROM and executed. • This gives the processor access to storage. • The full operating system is loaded from storage. • The operating system starts up. It runs all the time the computer is switched on.		*5.1 Functions of an operating system*
6	An interrupt is a signal that stops the current instruction from being executed. It points the processor to a new instruction in memory.		*5.1 Functions of an operating system*

5.2 Computer languages

Question number	Answer	Is your answer correct? (Tick)	If you did not give the correct answer, reread this section
1	Machine code consists of binary numbers that stand for actions that can be carried out by the processor. They can be written using hexadecimal. In either form the instructions are difficult to read and write so this system is rarely used to create new software directly.		*5.2 Programming languages*
2	Assembly language has short words instead of the binary or hexadecimal numbers of machine code.		*5.2 Low-level languages*
3	Compared to high-level languages, assembly language is more similar to the instruction set of the computer. This means assembly language programs are shorter and more efficient. However, assembly language is more difficult to use than most high-level languages and the programs will often only work with one make of computer.		*5.2 Low-level languages*
4	Program code has to be translated into machine code before it can be executed. This is because the processor only understands machine code.		*5.2 Low-level languages*
5	A compiled program is converted into a complete file of machine code. The machine code file can be loaded and run to carry out the instructions. An interpreted program is translated one line at a time into machine code. The code is immediately executed but not saved.		*5.2 High-level languages*
6	A programmer should know a range of different computer languages because different languages have different strengths and weaknesses that suit them to different uses. Programmers choose the language that is most suitable for a given task.		*5.2 High-level languages*
7	Advantages of compiled languages: • You end up with an executable file. • You can sell or share the file. • Anyone can run the file. Disadvantages of compiled languages: • You must compile the program to make a new executable file every time you make a change. • Versions of the file can get mixed up.		*5.2 High-level languages*
8	Advantage of interpreted languages: • If you make a change to your code, you can run the program and see the effect right away. Disadvantages of interpreted languages: • The program will not run unless you have the interpreter on your computer. • There is no executable file to sell or share.		*5.2 High-level languages*

6 Security

6.1 Security threats

Question number	Answer	Is your answer correct? (Tick)	If you did not give the correct answer, reread this section
1	Data integrity means the data is not lost, deleted, changed or corrupted.		*6.1 Data security*
2	Data privacy means the data is not seen, copied or altered by unauthorised people.		*6.1 Data security*
3	Data loss – the data is completely gone. Data corruption – the data is changed so it is not accurate and/or usable. Unauthorised access – someone who doesn't have permission can see or change the data.		*6.1 Data security*
4	Internal threats are as follows: • Hardware faults can occur. Hardware breaks or does not work and this damages the data. You can reduce hardware faults by buying good quality equipment, having fire protection measures, and training people to use equipment properly. • Software faults can occur. Software breaks or works wrongly and data is lost or changed. Software faults can be prevented by buying good-quality software and training people to use it properly. • Malpractice can be a threat. Malpractice means not doing work properly. Often malpractice involves the human users of a computer system making mistakes. Good training and support can reduce malpractice. • Crime can be a threat. Crime involves deliberate intention to cause harm. Crime by employees can be reduced by good recruitment and management of staff.		*6.1 Security threats*
5	There are many external threats to data. Some examples are floods, earthquakes and power cuts. Physical measures can include independent power supply and protective building design. All data should be backed up. External attacks include crime, fraud, malware and attack from hackers. Company security policies such as passwords and ID cards aim to protect systems from external attacks.		*6.1 Security threats*

Question number	Answer	Is your answer correct? (Tick)	If you did not give the correct answer, reread this section
6	There are many examples of malpractice. They include: • leaving the computer logged on and unattended • telling someone else your password • downloading software from the Internet. Staying logged on or disclosing passwords can give unauthorised people access to computer systems. Downloading software can put malware onto the computer system.		*6.1 Malpractice and crime*
7	Pharming is setting up a fake website that looks like an official company site. Criminals do this to get your passwords and other details from you.		*6.1 Online attacks*
8	Phishing is sending a fake email that looks like an official communication. Criminals do this to get your passwords and other details from you.		*6.1 Online attacks*
9	A distributed denial of service (DDoS) is a way of harming a company's computer services. It works by flooding the computer with many requests or messages that seem to be sent from hundreds of different addresses. This makes it harder to block them all.		*6.1 Online attacks*

6.2 Security protection

Question number	Answer	Is your answer correct? (Tick)	If you did not give the correct answer, reread this section
1	Identity can be proved through use of password, biometrics and ID cards.		*6.2 Proof of identity*
2	A company uses more than one method because all the methods have strengths and weaknesses. Combining them provides extra checks.		*6.2 Proof of identity*
3	A firewall checks all data passing between a LAN and an Internet connection. It only transmits data that passes security checks.		*6.2 Firewalls*
4	A proxy server stores Internet content on a local (nearby) server. This means access is quicker and more secure.		*6.2 Firewalls*

Question number	Answer	Is your answer correct? (Tick)	If you did not give the correct answer, reread this section
5	Protocols are standard rules for communication. Security protocols are standards that ensure data is transmitted securely to trusted sites.		*6.2 Security protocols*
6	A handshake allows two computers to share proof that they are authentic. This is typically verified by an electronic certificate issued by a trusted certification authority (CA).		*6.2 Security protocols*
7	Encryption means turning plain text into encrypted text. An encryption key is used in the process.		*6.2 Encryption*
8	In asymmetric encryption only the encryption key is shared over the Internet. The decryption key is kept private. This improves security because the key is not transmitted over the Internet.		*6.2 Encryption*
9	There are many valid examples. One example is e-commerce, which relies on the secure transmission of payment details to trusted retailers.		*6.2 Security examples*

7 Ethics

Question number	Answer	Is your answer correct? (Tick)	If you did not give the correct answer, reread this section
1	Illegal behaviour is punishable by laws. Unethical behaviour is wrong but it may not be covered by laws.		*7.1 Ethics*
2	Greater use of computers has brought in new crimes and new ways to commit crimes, such as phishing or pharming to steal people's identity and/or their money. Laws need to be changed to cover these new types of crime.		*7.1 Ethics*
3	IPR stands for "intellectual property rights". It gives people rights over their own creative works. Copyright laws prevent people from making copies of works without permission. These laws ensure that makers of creative content are rewarded for their work.		*7.1 Copyright*

Question number	Answer	Is your answer correct? (Tick)	If you did not give the correct answer, reread this section
4	Plagiarism means taking someone else's work and pretending it is your own. Computers have made it easier to plagiarise because they have made it easier to take copies of people's work.		7.1 Copyright
5	Free software is open source software that you can use, copy, adapt and even re-sell. It may not be free to buy. Freeware is software that is free of charge – you don't pay for it. It is not in the public domain. The owners retain their IPR. Shareware is similar to freeware. It is not in the public domain. It is free of charge but there are often restrictions on the work you can do with shareware – to remove these restrictions you must pay for the software.		7.1 Free software
6	Black hat hackers (also known as crackers) break into computer systems without permission. White hat hackers break into computer systems with permission, to test the security. Grey hat hackers may break into systems without permission. However, they may not do any damage.		7.1 Hackers and crackers

8 Programming

8.1 Introduction to programming

Question number	Answer	Is your answer correct? (Tick)	If you did not give the correct answer, reread this section
1	An IDE is software that lets you prepare your program code and save it as a file.		8.1 Introduction to Python
2	Three features of an IDE are: • use of colour to show different types of code • a command to run the program code • error messages.		8.1 Introduction to Python
3	An algorithm describes a set of steps to solve a problem.		8.1 Algorithms
4	There are many reasons why a programmer might write an algorithm. Three examples are: to plan, record and share their program method.		8.1 Algorithms

Question number	Answer	Is your answer correct? (Tick)	If you did not give the correct answer, reread this section
5	The output of the program is the useful result of the program, and it is what the client requires.		*8.1 Algorithms*
6	A flowchart uses arrows to show the sequence of actions.		*8.1 Algorithms*
7	Pseudocode is different from a programming language because you cannot run the code to control the action of the computer.		*8.1 Algorithms*
8	Pseudocode is more similar to normal program code than flowcharts. It is easier to produce a neat clear version of pseudocode. It does not need special graphics software to prepare pseudocode. It takes up less space than a flowchart.		*8.1 Algorithms*

8.2 Begin coding

Question number	Answer
1	Example: ```\n## This program inputs a decimal value\n## Then shows it as a percentage\nDecimalvalue = input("enter a decimal value ")\nDecimalvalue = float(Decimalvalue)\nPercentage = Decimalvalue * 100\nprint(Percentage, "%")\n```
2	```\nREAD Decimalvalue\nPercentage ← Decimalvalue * 100\nPRINT Percentage\n```
3	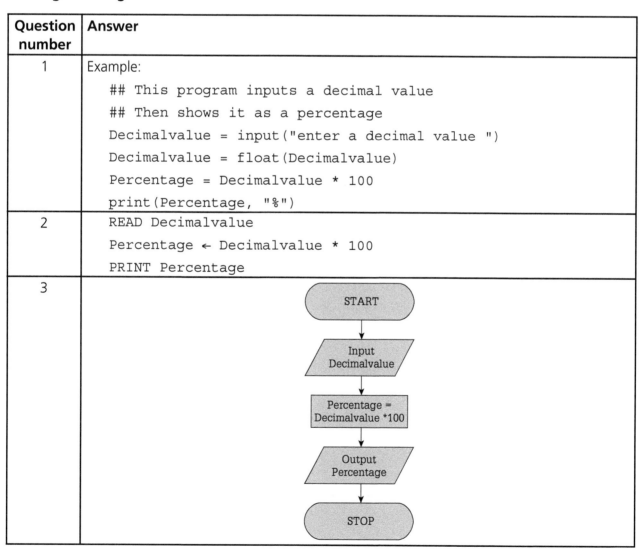

8.3 Selection

Question number	Answer

1	There is more than one way to solve this problem. Here is one example.
	
	``
	## Find largest
	A = input("enter the first number ")
	B = input("enter the second number ")
	A = int(A)
	B = int(B)
	if A > B:
	    Biggest = A
	else:
	    Biggest = B
	print("The biggest number is ", Biggest)
	``

2	

3	This algorithm matches the structure of the Python program shown in question 1. Can you think of another way to solve this problem?
	
	``
	READ A
	READ B
	IF A > B THEN
	    BIGGEST ← A
	ELSE
	    BIGGEST ← B
	ENDIF
	PRINT BIGGEST
	``

Question number	Answer
| 4 | ```
## CLASSIFY NUMBER
Number = input("enter a number value for testing ")
Number = float(Number)
if Number < 0:
    print("The number is a negative value")
elif Number ==0:
    print("The number is 0")
else:
    print("The number is greater than zero")
``` |
| 5 | ```
READ Number
CASE Number OF
    <0: PRINT "The number is a negative value"
    0: PRINT "The number is 0"
OTHERWISE
    PRINT "The number is greater than zero"
ENDCASE
``` |

8.4 Repetition

Question number	Answer
| 1 | ```
number = input("enter a number value ")
number = int(number)
factorial = 1
for i in range(1, number+1):
    factorial = factorial*i
print(number,"! = ",factorial)
``` |
| 2 | ```
READ Number
Factorial ← 1
FOR i ← 1 TO Number
    Factorial ← Factorial * i
NEXT i
PRINT Factorial
``` |

Question number	Answer
3	
| 4 | ```
## email check
version1 = input("Enter your email address ")
version2 = input("Enter the address again ")
while version1 != version2:
    version2 = input("Does not match, enter again ")
print("Email entered")
``` |
| 5 | ```
READ Version1
READ Version2
WHILE Version1 <> Version2 DO
    READ Version2
ENDWHILE
PRINT "Email entered"
``` |
| 6 | ```
READ Version1
REPEAT
    READ Version2
UNTIL Version1 = Version2
PRINT "Email entered"
``` |
```

Question number	Answer
7	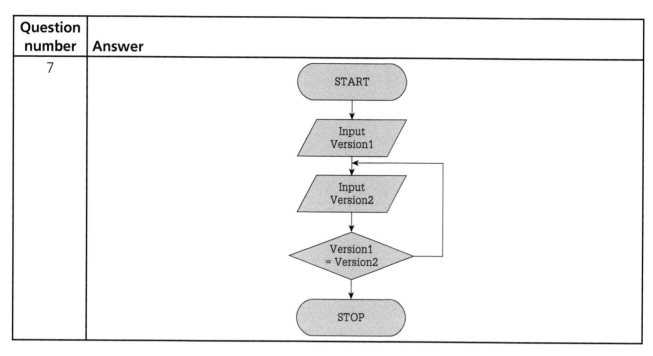

8.5 Data structures

Question number	Answer
| 1 | ```
PatientList = []
for i in range(7):
    PatientName = input("Add a new patient name: ")
    PatientList.append(PatientName)
``` |
| 2 | ```
PatientList = []
for i in range(7):
    PatientName = input("Add a new patient name: ")
    PatientList.append(PatientName)
for i in range(7):
    print(PatientList[i])
``` |
| 3 | ```
Patientlist[1:7]
FOR i ← 1 TO 7
    INPUT Name
    Patientlist[i]← Name
Next i
FOR i ← 1 TO 7
    PRINT Patientlist[i]
Next i
``` |
```

Question number	Answer
| 4 | ```python
PatientList = []
Continue = "Y"
while Continue == "Y":
    PatientName = input("Type the patient name: ")
    PatientList.append(PatientName)
    Continue = input("Add another? (Y/N): ")
listlength = len(PatientList)
for i in range(listlength):
    print(PatientList[i])
``` |

9 Solution development

9.1 Worked examples

Question number	Answer	Is your answer correct? (Tick)	If you did not give the correct answer, reread this section
1	This pseudocode algorithm counts how many. It counts how many times the user enters the letter "X".		*9.1 Count how many*
2	This pseudocode algorithm adds up a total using a counter-controlled loop. At the start of the program the user says how many values will be entered. Then the values are added together to give a total.		*9.1 Calculate a total*
| 3 | ```
Sum ← 0
FOR i ← 1 TO 5
    READ Mark
    Sum ← Sum + Mark
NEXT i
Average = Sum / 5
PRINT Average
``` | | *9.1 Calculate an average* |
| 4 | ```
REPEAT
    READ Try1
    READ Try2
UNTIL Try1 = Try2
Address ← Try1
``` | | *9.1 Verification* |
```

Question number	Answer	Is your answer correct? (Tick)	If you did not give the correct answer, reread this section

5	There are many correct answers. Here is an example.
	
	``
	print("Enter date of birth")
	Day = input("Day: ")
	Month = input("Month: ")
	Year = input ("Year: ")
	Month = int(Month)
	while Month > 12:
	    Month = input("Month
	    1-12: ")
	``
			9.1 Validation

6	There are many correct answers. You can include length and range checks. You can use `elif`. Test your program to make sure it works properly.		*9.1 Validation*

9.2 Testing and evaluation

Question number	Answer
1	You could give the answer A, B, C or X. These are all examples of normal correct data. If you entered A (for example) you would expect to see your account balance on the screen.
2	There are lots of correct answers. Any letter except A, B, C or X is abnormal data. Any number value is abnormal data. If you entered abnormal data you would expect to see an error message. You might have another chance to enter a menu choice.
3	There are lots of correct answers. Some examples are: • normal data: a typical money amount such as $100. • extreme data: a very large money amount such as $1 000 000. • abnormal data: something that is not a number such as "abc".
4	The test table with these examples is shown below. Your table will show your own example tests.
5	The example test is abnormal data. The software should not accept this data. It should show an error message. This did not happen. Therefore the test shows that the programmer must make improvements to the software.
6	Here is the completed test table showing all four tests.

Test number	Purpose of test	Test data	Expected output	Actual result	Analysis
1	Test cash withdrawal using normal data	100	£100 is given by the machine. Account balance goes down by 100.	Account balance goes down by 100.	The software is effective.
2	Test cash withdrawal using extreme data	1 000 000	The message appears saying "Not enough money in your account".	The message appears saying "Not enough money in your account".	The software is effective.
3	Test cash withdrawal using abnormal data	abc	The message "Not a valid amount" appears.	The message "Not a valid amount" appears.	The software is effective.
4	Test login to cash machine	abc	The message "Not a valid passcode" appears.	The user is logged in to the system.	The software is not effective. It must be improved.

9.3 Developing algorithms

Question number	Answer	Is your answer correct? (Tick)	If you did not give the correct answer, reread this section
1	A trace table is used to test and evaluate an algorithm. A trace table has a column for each variable in the algorithm. Before making a trace table you should number every line of a pseudocode algorithm and every box of a flowchart. To simplify a trace table, only include rows where a variable changes value.		*9.3 Trace tables*
2	<table><tr><th>Line</th><th>A</th><th>B</th><th>C</th></tr><tr><td>1</td><td>0</td><td></td><td></td></tr><tr><td>2</td><td>0</td><td>Y</td><td></td></tr><tr><td>4</td><td>0</td><td>Y</td><td>50</td></tr><tr><td>5</td><td>50</td><td>Y</td><td>50</td></tr><tr><td>6</td><td>50</td><td>Y</td><td>50</td></tr><tr><td>4</td><td>50</td><td>Y</td><td>122</td></tr><tr><td>5</td><td>122</td><td>Y</td><td>122</td></tr><tr><td>6</td><td>122</td><td>N</td><td>122</td></tr></table> The final output is 122.		*9.3 Trace tables (loops)*

Question number	Answer	Is your answer correct? (Tick)	If you did not give the correct answer, reread this section
3	The algorithm finds the largest in a series of numbers.		*9.3 Analyse algorithms*
| 4 | ```
1   READ A
2   READ B
3   C = A/B
4   PRINT C
``` | | *9.3 Create an algorithm* |
| 5 | If the second value that the user enters is a zero then the run-time error "divide by zero" will occur.

To fix this error add a validation check that blocks any input that is 0. | | *9.3 Find errors in algorithms* |
| 6 | There are several correct solutions. Here is an example.<br><br>```
1   READ A
2   READ B
3   IF B = 0 THEN
4     PRINT "0 not allowed"
5     C = 0
6   ELSE
7     C = A/B
8   ENDIF
9   PRINT C
``` | | |

9.4 Development methods

Question number	Answer	Is your answer correct? (Tick)	If you did not give the correct answer, reread this section
1	Top-down programing means breaking down a programming task into smaller tasks. The different tasks are completed separately and then the smaller programs are fitted together to make a complete solution.		*9.4 Top-down programming*
2	You should give as many as you can from this list: • You can plan the task as a series of sub-tasks. • You can break a large difficult task down into smaller and easier tasks. • The different tasks can be given to different people in the team. • Each sub-system can be tested before they are all fitted together.		*9.4 Top-down programming*
3	You might include these sub-systems: • The user sets or resets the alarm time. • The user sets or resets the current time. • The user turns the alarm on and off. • The clock shows the current time. • If the alarm is on and it is the alarm time, the application make a noise.		*9.4 Top-down programming*
4	Several different structure diagrams could answer this question. Here is an example. 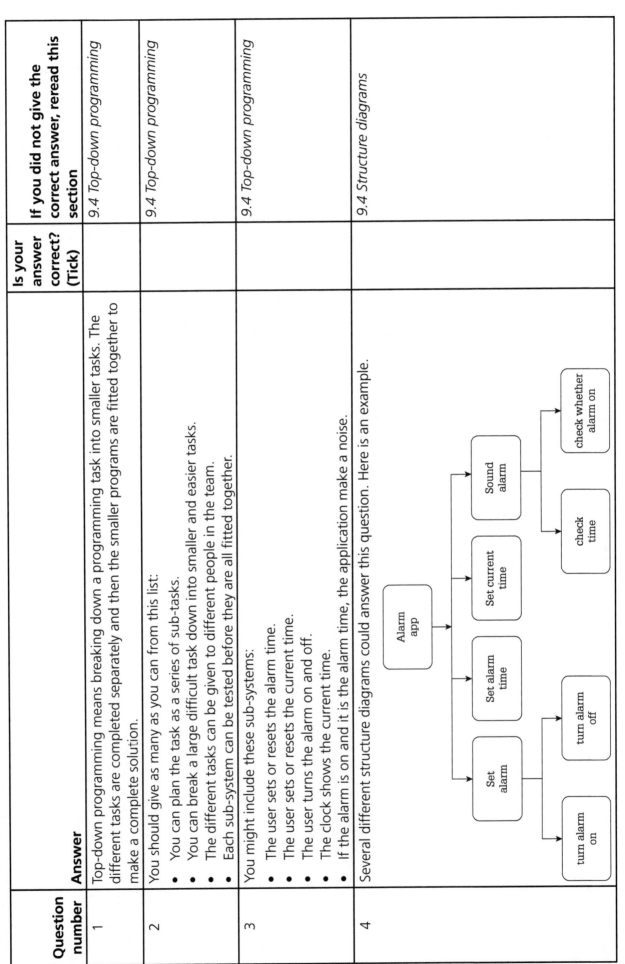		*9.4 Structure diagrams*

Question number	Answer	Is your answer correct? (Tick)	If you did not give the correct answer, reread this section
5	A well-designed structure diagram has these features: • Every function of the software is included in the chart. • Every function appears once only. • The sub-systems are distinct with no overlap. • The sub-systems are the simplest possible parts.		9.4 *Structure diagrams*
6	Some functions are so useful that they are part of standard program code. These are called predefined functions.		9.4 *Code libraries*
7	Programmers make their own procedures and functions. They sometimes collect together many useful sub-routines that do similar things. They store them in a large file called a module.		9.4 *Code libraries*
8	Modules can be stored all together as a code library of useful routines. Programmers often make code libraries freely available.		9.4 *Code libraries*
9	Reusing sub-routines saves time and reduces work. The modules are tried and tested so there is less chance of error.		9.4 *Code libraries*

10 Databases

10.1 Database design

Question number	Answer	Is your answer correct? (Tick)	If you did not give the correct answer, reread this section
1	Databases store facts. The facts refer to things or people. They are called entities. The entities in this table are islands.		*10.1 Records and fields*
2	A record is all the facts about a single entity. There are eight records in this table.		*10.1 Records and fields*
3	A field stores a single fact about the entities. There are five fields in this table.		*10.1 Records and fields*
4	<table><tr><td>Field name</td><td>Data type</td></tr><tr><td>Code</td><td>Text</td></tr><tr><td>Island's name</td><td>Text</td></tr><tr><td>Area (sq miles)</td><td>Number</td></tr><tr><td>Country</td><td>Text</td></tr><tr><td>Population</td><td>Number</td></tr></table>		*10.1 Data types*
5	A primary key will identify each record because it is unique in the table. I would use the code field as the primary key. I would not use population or area because there might be two islands with the same area or population. I would not use the name of the island because that could change over time. I would not use country because you can have two islands that belong to the same country (e.g. Canada).		*10.1 Primary key*

10.2 Database queries

Question number	Answer
1	<table><tr><td></td><td>Code</td><td>Name</td><td>Area</td><td>Country</td><td>Population</td></tr><tr><td>Table</td><td>Islands</td><td>Islands</td><td>Islands</td><td>Islands</td><td>Islands</td></tr><tr><td>Show</td><td></td><td>✔</td><td></td><td></td><td>✔</td></tr><tr><td>Sort</td><td></td><td></td><td>Ascending</td><td></td><td></td></tr><tr><td>Criteria</td><td></td><td></td><td></td><td>= "Canada"</td><td></td></tr></table>
2	<table><tr><td>Island's name</td><td>Population</td></tr><tr><td>Victoria Island</td><td>1875</td></tr><tr><td>Baffin Island</td><td>10 745</td></tr></table>

3		Code	Name	Area	Country	Population	
	Table	Islands	Islands	Islands	Islands	Islands	
	Show		✔	✔		✔	
	Sort		Ascending				
	Criteria					>1 000 000	

4	Island's name	Area (sq miles)	Population
	Borneo	288 869	19 800 000
	Honshu	87 200	103 000 000
	Madagascar	226 917	25 000 000
	New Guinea	303 381	11 000 000
	Sumatra	171 069	50 000 000

5		Code	Name	Area	Country	Population	
	Table	Islands	Islands	Islands	Islands	Islands	
	Show	✔	✔	✔	✔	✔	
	Sort						
	Criteria			>100 000			
	AND					<100 000	

6	Code	Island's name	Area (sq miles)	Country	Population
	01	Greenland	822 700	Greenland and Denmark	56 000
	05	Baffin Island	195 928	Canada	10 745

Answers to exam preparation and exam-style questions

1 Data representation

Exam preparation

1. **a** Binary means two.
   b A binary digit can be either a 0 or a 1. It is often shortened to the word bit.
   c Hexadecimal means 16.
   d There are 16 hexadecimal digits: 0, 1, 2, 3, 4, 5, 6, 7, 8, 9, A, B, C, D, E, F.

Exam-style questions

1. **a** AE2D
   b

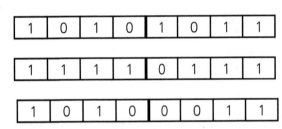

1	0	1	0	1	0	1	1

1	1	1	1	0	1	1	1

   c

1	0	1	0	0	0	1	1

   d 128 + 32 + 2 + 1 = 163
2. **a** When a file is stored, usually if it is larger, it has more information to represent the detail of the file contents. This means that the stored file would have a higher quality. Therefore, if the file size is smaller, the file stored is more likely to be of lower quality.
   b The image file may be compressed so that it is reduced in size to be used in a web page. This means that some of the detail which is repeated in the image would be removed. For example, if there is a large block of the same colour, one pixel is stored along with a number to say how many repetitions there are.
   c A text file may have its size reduced by using lossless compression. In this case repeated words or phrases may be substituted with a code. When the file is decompressed, the original text is substituted back into the file.

2 Communications and the Internet

Exam preparation

1. **a** Simplex communications travel in one direction only; for example, listening to the radio.
   b Duplex communications travel in both directions at the same time so that conversations can take place; for example, using a telephone.
   c HTML stands for Hypertext Mark-up Language. It is the language used to create web pages and to control the layout, structure and appearance of the web pages.
   d HTTP stands for Hypertext Transfer Protocol. It is used to define links between web pages and allows web pages to appear in a browser.

Exam-style questions

1. **a** Serial transmission uses a single wire to transmit data, so only one bit at a time is transmitted. Parallel transmission has multiple wires transmitting data at the same time – typically eight – so a whole byte may be transmitted at the same time.
   b An advantage of parallel transmission is that it could transmit data more quickly, as it transmits multiple bits at the same time. A disadvantage is that, over longer distances, some of the bits

may arrive at the destination quicker than others, causing the data to be skewed. Parallel transmission is used for short distance communication such as in a data bus inside a CPU.

c An advantage of serial transmission is that the single wire allows it to be used for long distance transmissions without suffering for interference. A disadvantage is that transmission times may be longer due to data being sent one bit at a time. Serial transmission is used for long distance communication such as connecting peripherals (such as printers) to a computer system.

d Parity

0	1	1	0	0	0	1	1
1	0	0	0	0	0	1	0
0	1	0	1	0	1	0	1

2.

a	Virus	Trojan	Spyware
b i	Self- replicating program	Disguised as a legitimate file such as an image	Records keystrokes and sends them back to its creator
b ii	Can cause damage to other files on your computer	Can allow hackers to gain access to your data and steal personal information	Can allow your data to be analysed and give criminals access to your bank details
b iii	Use anti-virus software	Do not open email attachments from unknown sources	Use anti-virus software

c A firewall is a piece of hardware or software that blocks unauthorised access to your computer system while permitting outward communication.

3 The processor

Exam preparation

1. a    **b**

c Input ——▷o—— Output   **d**

e    **f** A —⊐Do— Output

Exam-style questions

1. a NOT and AND gates, when combines, form a NAND gate.

b

OR Gate		
A	**B**	**Q**
0	0	0
0	1	1
1	0	1
1	1	1

XOR Gate		
A	**B**	**Q**
0	0	0
0	1	1
1	0	1
1	1	0

With the OR gate, there is an output if either one of the inputs, **or both of them,** are set to 1. With an XOR gate there is an output if either of the inputs, **but not both,** are set to 1.

c

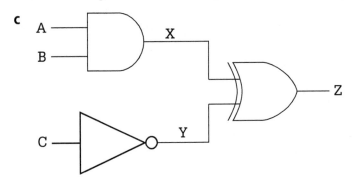

2. a i A register is used to store data before it is processed.
   ii A bus is used to transport data from one part of the CPU to another.
   iii The Arithmetic and Logic Unit (ALU) performs calculations in the CPU.
   b The fetch-execute cycle is made up of three elements:
   Fetch: the control unit fetches a Machine Code instruction from main memory.
   Decode: the control unit decodes the instruction so it knows what action to carry out.
   Execute: the control unit sends the instruction to the ALU. The ALU carries out the action.

4 Hardware

Exam preparation

1. a Input – data is put in to the computer system.
   b Output – data is taken out of the computer system.
   c Storage – data is stored in the computer system either permanently or temporarily.

Exam-style questions

1. a

Keyboard	Mouse
Advantages:	**Advantages:**
Intuitive to use Supplied with a computer system	Easy to control the mouse pointer to click on objects or to draw with Inexpensive to buy
Disadvantages:	**Disadvantages:**
Difficult to use to draw graphics Need to be able to type to use efficiently	Awkward to use to enter text Don't work well on all desktop surfaces

b Barcodes are a type of electronic data entry system that allow a code number to be scanned, which in turn, allows a computer system to find the details of the item in its database. This is useful for entering sales in an EPOS system or for identifying a product in a stock control system.

Optical Character Recognition is a different type of automatic data entry system that is used to recognise handwritten or manually typed text and convert it into computer input. It sometimes fails to recognise some poorly defined characters, but it allows data for which there is no electronic copy to be edited.

c **i** One advantage of an infra-red touch screen is that it can be 'touched' with any object e.g. a finger, a glove or a pen. It is, however, a more expensive type of screen.

ii Another type of touch screen technology is called resistive. In this case it uses two thin layers that conduct electricity. When you touch the screen, you push the layers together causing an electrical signal to be sent, matching the place you touched the screen.

Infra-red technology works with a grid of invisible beams. When you touch the screen, you break the beam and the screen is able to determine where the break happened.

2. a

i Inkjet Printer	**ii** Laser Printer
Benefits:	**Benefits:**
Small and quiet machine	Very fast printing – page printing
Inexpensive to purchase	Economical print cost per page
Drawbacks:	**Drawbacks:**
Prints out line by line so can be slow for large print tasks	High initial cost
Ink cartridges are expensive to replace and don't last very long	Large, heavy and bulky machine
Use	**Use**
Used in homes or small businesses	Used in larger organisations or schools

b Objects can be designed on a computer screen using CAD software.

i Objects can be designed quickly.

Objects can be altered if necessary before an expensive prototype is built.

ii Solid output can be made using a 3D Printer or a 3D laser Cutter.

3. a

RAM	ROM
Features:	**Features:**
Very fast to access	Permanent memory programmed at the factory
Contents lost when the power is switched off	Usually makes up a small proportion of the primary storage
Purpose:	**Purpose:**
Used to store programs and data while they are being executed	Stores the BIOS to allow a computer system to start up

b

i Hard Disk Drive	**ii** DVD RW	**iii** Solid State Drive
Advantage	**Advantage**	**Advantage**
High capacity storage	Contents can be altered	More permanent storage
Disadvantage	**Disadvantage**	**Disadvantage**
Can be damaged by magnetic interference	Access is not as quick as some other types	Capacity doesn't yet match magnetic disks
Desktop computer secondary storage	Backup of data files in a home setting	Laptop computer secondary storage

5 Software

Exam preparation

1. **a** Applications software are the programs you use on your computer. They are also referred to as 'apps' and are the programs that make the computer useful to you.

   b Systems software is the software that controls your computer; that makes it run.

Exam-style questions

1. **a** The operations carried out by an operating system (OS) are: controlling hardware; user interface; loading and running applications; and handling errors and problems.

   b

Controlling hardware	User interface
i The OS lets the CPU communicate with the peripherals e.g. monitor, printer	**i** The User interface hides the complexity of the computer from the user and allows the computer to be used
ii Allows a document to be sent to the printer for printing	**ii** Graphical user interface (GUI)

Loading and running applications	Handling errors and problems
i The OS will open and run an application once it has been selected by the user	**i** The OS responds to errors such as hardware failure or mistakes made by the user
ii Use of mouse to click on an icon using a GUI	**ii** Printer running out of paper

   c An interrupt is a signal that stops the current instruction from being executed. It points the processor to a new instruction in memory.

2. **a** A high level language uses common English words making it easier for the programmer to understand; whereas low level languages use either binary codes or mnemonics, which make them more difficult for the programmer to understand.

   b The two types of program used to translate a program into a form the computer can understand are: a compiler and an interpreter.

   c

Compiler
i A compiler translates the whole program into machine code before it executes. Once a program is compiled, it does not need to be compiled again unless it is altered.
ii A compiled program executes very quickly as it is already in machine code.
iii Some programs can take a long time to compile before you can see the results of the program.
Interpreter
i An interpreter translates one line of code into machine code at a time. It therefore executes immediately.
ii Using an interpreter allows you to see your program working much more quickly as each line executes as soon as it is translated.
iii Programs using an interpreter are not as efficient as compiled programs, as each line is translated into machine code every time it is run, which if loops have been used, could be many times.

6 Security

Exam preparation

1. **a** Keeping data private means only allowing access to those with permission to see it.
   b Data integrity is making sure the data is complete and undamaged.
   b Data security is ensuring the privacy and integrity of data on computer systems.

Exam-style questions

1. **a** Pharming is where a piece of malicious code or malware is installed on a person's computer. This code redirects the user to a fraudulent website that resembles a legitimate one. When the user enters personal information such as password details, these details are stolen.
   b Phishing is where an email is sent to a user containing an attachment. The attachment is fraudulent and opens up to a fake website resembling a legitimate one, such as the user's bank. The user is asked for login details and if they are entered they are stolen, thereby giving fraudulent access to their bank account.
   c Hacking is when an unauthorised user accesses your computer files for some illicit purpose. It could mean that they wish to steal some information, or they may cause damage to your files.

2. **a** Authentication is the process by which a computer program confirms that a user has the right to log in to it; that it is dealing with an authorised user.
   b

Use of Passwords	Use of Biometrics	Use of ID cards
Advantage	**Advantage**	**Advantage**
Relatively simple to set up with program code	Very secure as it is difficult to steal someone's fingerprint, for example	Dual purpose system that can be read by a person as well as a special card reader
Disadvantage	**Disadvantage**	**Disadvantage**
Passwords need to be strong or they can be easy to guess	Biometric readers are needed, which can be expensive	ID cards can be lost or stolen

3. **a** Three functions of a firewall are:
   i Checking that all incoming data meets a given set of criteria.
   ii Blocking incoming data that do not meet the specified criteria.
   iii Protection against threats such as Denial of Service (DOS) attacks.
   b Encryption is used to prevent data being read by unauthorised users. It is a process by which a key is applied to the data to create scrambled or cypher text before transmission. When it is received it is turned back into plain text by the receiver using a decryption key.

7 Ethics

Exam preparation

1. Computer ethics is the study of right and wrong in the context of using a computer. It is ensuring that your use of the computer is ethical so that you do not cause harm to others or break any laws.

Exam-style questions

1 **a** Copyright applies to different media types including text, music, video and software. If it is in copyright, it means that you cannot make a copy of it or any part of it, excluding 'fair use', without permission.

b The copyright holder has intellectual property rights over anything they have created with their own ideas. It means they may receive payment, known as royalties, for someone else to have a copy of their material.

2. a Free software is software in which the user has access to the source code. They are allowed to modify the code and pass it on to others without breaking copyright laws.

b Freeware is software that users are allowed to download and use for free, but they are not allowed to alter it in any way.

c Shareware is a type of software that can be downloaded and tried out for free, but in order to carry on using it after a certain time, or in order to use a full version of the software, they have to pay.

3. Some hackers are known as white hat hackers. These are usually computer users who enjoy a challenge and like to break into computer systems to see if they can, without a malicious intent. They are often employed by companies to test out security systems, so effectively, they try to break into a computer system <u>with</u> permission.

8 Programming

Exam preparation

1. a IDE means Integrated Development Environment. It is software that helps you prepare your program code and save it as a file.

b An algorithm describes a set of steps used to solve a problem.

c A flowchart is a diagram used to show an algorithm in a graphical format using a standard set of symbols joined together by arrows.

d Pseudocode represents an algorithm in a format similar to program code.

Exam-style questions

1.
```
REPEAT

        PRINT "Enter a new password"

        INPUT NewPassword1

        PRINT "Please re-enter your new password"

        INPUT NewPassword2

    UNTIL NewPassword1 = NewPassword2

    Password ← NewPassword1

    PRINT "Your password is confirmed as", Password
```

2.

Data Entered	Data Type
25.00	Real or Float
Smithson	String
Yes	Boolean
100	Integer
X	Char or Character

3. Variable: Weight
Constant: MaxWeight = 100

9 Solution development

Exam preparation

1. **a** Verification means to check whether an input value that has been entered matches the one that was intended to be entered.
   b Validation means to check that the value entered is possible or sensible.

Exam-style questions

1. Test data for a program expecting you to enter 5 whole numbers between 0 and 100:

a	5, 25, 30, 50, 75	0, 0, 100, 0, 100	25, 10, 7, 125, a7
b i	This is a set of normal data, within the range specified	This is a set of extreme data, on the boundaries of acceptability	This set contains abnormal data which is out of range and of the wrong data type
b ii	The data should be accepted	The data should be accepted	The data should be rejected

2. **a**

Count	Total	Max	LoopCount	Number	OUTPUT
0	0	10			
1	2		1	2	
2	27		2	25	
3	30		3	3	
4	31		4	1	
5	47		5	16	
6	52		6	5	
7	60		7	8	
8	72		8	12	
9	80		9	8	
10	90		10	10	9

   b The purpose of the algorithm is to allow ten numbers to be entered. These numbers are added together as they are entered, then, at the end, their average is the output.

10 Databases

Exam preparation

1. **a** A field is one of the columns in the data table. It is one fact about the data.
   b A record is one row of the data table. It holds a piece of data about each data fact for a single entity.
   c A primary key is a special kind of field. Its contents must be unique for each record so that a specific record can be identified.

Exam-style questions

1. It is most appropriate to choose the Symbol field as the primary key for this database because each entry is unique to the record. In this database, several of the fields contain unique data, however, the data entered in the Symbol field are short, making entry errors less likely and are easily

recognisable for the record they represent.

2.

Field	Data Type
Atomic Weight	Number
Name	Text
Symbol	Text
Melting point (°C)	Number

3.

	Name	Symbol	Atomic Number	Atomic Weight	Boiling Point (°C)
Field:					
Table:	PERIODIC TABLE	PERIODIC TABLE	PERIODIC TABLE	PERIODIC TABLE	PERIODIC TABLE
Sort:	Ascending				
Show:	☑	☑	☑	☑	☑
Criteria:					>0
or:					